GETTING GREAT RESULTS FROM YOUR
ice cream machine

GETTING GREAT RESULTS FROM YOUR
ice cream machine

Simple ways to create fabulous iced desserts, with more than 80 step-by-step recipes shown in over 550 stunning photographs

**Joanna Farrow
and Sara Lewis**

southwater

This edition is published by Southwater, an imprint of
Anness Publishing Ltd, Hermes House, 88–89 Blackfriars Road,
London SE1 8HA; tel. 020 7401 2077; fax 020 7633 9499

www.southwaterbooks.com; www.annesspublishing.com

If you like the images in this book and would like to investigate using
them for publishing, promotions or advertising, please visit our
website www.practicalpictures.com for more information.

UK agent: The Manning Partnership Ltd; tel. 01225 478444;
  fax 01225 478440; sales@manning-partnership.co.uk
UK distributor: Grantham Book Services Ltd; tel. 01476 541080;
  fax 01476 541061; orders@gbs.tbs-ltd.co.uk
North American agent/distributor: National Book Network;
  tel. 301 459 3366; fax 301 429 5746; www.nbnbooks.com
Australian agent/distributor: Pan Macmillan Australia;
  tel. 1300 135 113; fax 1300 135 103;
  customer.service@macmillan.com.au
New Zealand agent/distributor: David Bateman Ltd;
  tel. (09) 415 7664; fax (09) 415 8892

Publisher: Joanna Lorenz
Senior managing editor: Conor Kilgallon
Editors: Lucy Doncaster and Margaret Malone
Copy editors: Jenni Fleetwood and Jan Cutler
Designers: Bill Mason and Luise Roberts
Photography: Gus Filgate, William Lingwood and Craig Robertson
Home economists: Joanna Farrow, Annabel Ford and Lucy McKelvie
Styling: Penny Markham and Helen Trent
Production controller: Steve Lang

ETHICAL TRADING POLICY
At Anness Publishing we believe that business should be conducted
in an ethical and ecologically sustainable way, with respect for the
environment and a proper regard to the replacement of the natural
resources we employ.

As a publisher, we use a lot of wood pulp to make high-quality
paper for printing, and that wood commonly comes from spruce
trees. We are therefore currently growing more than 500,000 trees
in two Scottish forest plantations near Aberdeen – Berrymoss (130
hectares/320 acres) and West Touxhill (125 hectares/305 acres).
The forests we manage contain twice the number of trees employed
each year in paper-making for our books.

Because of this ongoing ecological investment programme, you, as
our customer, can have the pleasure and reassurance of knowing
that a tree is being cultivated on your behalf to naturally replace the
materials used to make the book you are holding.

Our forestry programme is run in accordance with the UK Woodland
Assurance Scheme (UKWAS) and will be certified by the internationally
recognized Forest Stewardship Council (FSC). The FSC is a non-
government organization dedicated to promoting responsible
management of the world's forests. Certification ensures forests
are managed in an environmentally sustainable and socially
responsible basis. For further information about this scheme, go
to www.annesspublishing.com/trees

© Anness Publishing Ltd 2007

Previously published as part of a larger volume, *Ice Cream Machine*

Contents

Introduction

An ice cream maker is an invitation to indulgence. With this simple appliance you can create all your favourite flavours in your own kitchen, stocking the freezer for future feasts, making elaborate dinner-party sweets or simply impressing children or grandchildren with the magic transformation of basic ingredients into cool treats.

No longer will you need to dash to the supermarket for tubs of comfort food, or be unable to find your favourite sorbet when they are out of stock. An ice cream maker enables you to produce a wide range of delectable desserts, from the healthy refresher to the unashamedly sinful. What is more, because you decide which ingredients to use, you know precisely what the ice cream contains and can avoid additives or ingredients to which friends or family are intolerant.

Of course, making your own ice cream doesn't quite provide the instant gratification available to those who simply lever a lid off a tub, but the half hour or so it generally takes to produce the home-made product provides the ideal opportunity for musing on the pleasures ahead: the velvety texture, the sensuous way the ice cream slips off the spoon, the delicious coolness as it touches first your lips and then your throat, and finally the increasing intensity of the flavour as the ice cream warms to the heat of your body.

Ice cream is a winner with young and old alike. Statistically, the most enthusiastic consumers are those aged between two and twelve, and over the age of 45. Toddlers get the taste early, intrigued by what it is that gives older children such obvious satisfaction. The first scoop of ice cream usually ends up on the floor, but small children soon master the art of holding the cone steady while circumnavigating the icy globe, keeping the licks smooth and even so that not a drop is lost.

It is said that it takes about 50 licks to demolish a single scoop of ice cream, but this statistic presupposes a measured eater, neither a nibbler nor a greedy guzzler and certainly not one of those people who bite off the bottom of the cone and attack it at both ends.

BELOW: *Crisp wafers, bittersweet dark chocolate and crunchy nuts add flavour and texture to creamy scoops of home-made ice cream.*

ABOVE: *Elegant ice cream terrines make the perfect dinner-party dessert.*

For the older generation, ice cream evokes nostalgia for days when the sound of an ice cream van could spell refreshment on a warm summer afternoon: a neat rectangle of vanilla ice, perhaps sandwiched between two wafers, or a tub of Italian ice cream with its own little spoon.

Ice cream represents treat days and holidays, and today ice cream parlours are proliferating as never before. Home consumption of ice cream is also rocketing, and it has become a year-round treat. It is so convenient to open the freezer and reach for a lolly or a tub of ice cream or sorbet, and if you have made it yourself, you can indulge in a superior product that has probably cost you considerably less than the closest equivalent the supermarket can provide.

Ice creams, in all their guises, are the perfect conclusion to a meal, whether you are feeding the family or entertaining in a more formal fashion. Fruit sorbets and granitas are ideal for serving between courses to cleanse the palate during an elegant supper or a relaxed al fresco meal, while terrines – apparently elaborate but actually very easy to create – make an impressive finale to the most sophisticated dinner.

AN ICE CREAM LOVER'S GUIDE

You'll find recipes for everything from simple sorbets and granitas to luxurious terrines and even a Christmas Pudding Ice Cream in this comprehensive guide. First, though, there's a detailed reference section. We explore the history of this fascinating food, take you on a cook's tour of specialities from around the world, and offer advice on the best ingredients to use for perfect results every time. There is a comprehensive guide to the various types of ice cream machine available, plus plenty of tips for their use. Having made your ice cream, you'll want to know the best way to store and serve it, and these aspects are also explored fully. Instructions are given for making nut brittle, rippling raspberry jam and vanilla ice cream and making marbled mixtures. Sauces, cookies and flavourings are also described in detail.

A WORLD OF FLAVOURS

The recipe section includes ice creams and ices from the Mediterranean, Eastern Europe, India, the British Isles and the Americas. They range from a light and fresh Apple and Cider Water Ice to wickedly rich Classic Triple Chocolate Terrine. Among the more contemporary offerings are Pomegranate and Orange Flower Water Creams and Date and Tofu Ice, while for those who fancy an alcoholic kick there is a Bloody Mary Sorbet. Laced with vodka, it makes for intriguing after-dinner conversation.

Every recipe is illustrated with detailed, easy-to-follow step-by-step photographs, so that even the most inexperienced cook will feel confident about attempting every dessert, however complicated it may seem, and is guaranteed delicious home-made frozen desserts every time.

ABOVE: *Tangy Blackcurrant Sorbet is perfect after a rich meal.*

One of the obvious benefits of iced desserts is that they can be prepared in advance, so even those that require a bit of time and patience to put together can be made days or even weeks ahead. Brandied Fruit and Rice Ice Cream for instance, is a bit fiddly, as it requires you to soak dried fruit in brandy for several hours or overnight, then to make a creamy spiced rice pudding and a custard base, but the combination of flavours and textures is well worth the effort and the unusual ice cream is sure to be a hit with friends and family alike.

It is a good idea to make a large quantity of those iced desserts that use seasonal fruits, such as Raspberry Sorbet, Damson Water Ice or Strawberry and Rose Water Ice Cream, when the fruits are in season. Not only will the fruit be cheaper, but it will also have the best flavour, which can be savoured in the form of a delicious dessert throughout the year. Transforming the fruits into iced desserts is also a good way of making use of a glut of fruit, which might otherwise go to waste.

The book includes a chapter on cream-free, low-fat and low-sugar ices, many of which taste so rich and creamy that you may have difficulty convincing guests of their innocence. Blueberry and Honey Ripple Ice Cream, Honeyed Goat's Milk Gelato and Raspberry Sherbet are just some examples.

BELOW: *Light, crisp meringues and seasonal fruit complement simple ice creams.*

BELOW: *Iced Tiramisù will be loved by children and adults alike.*

The history of ice cream

No one knows for certain who produced the world's first ice cream, although it is probable that it was the Chinese who first developed the art of making frozen desserts in around AD618–97. They chilled fruit juices and tea, which led to their making primitive fruit-flavoured ices.

EARLY ICES

During Roman times, emperors such as Nero Claudius Caesar conceived the idea of serving a chilled dessert for a special feast. He is said to have sent his slaves into the mountains to gather fresh snow, which was dressed with honey and fruits and served as an early form of ice cream.

When Marco Polo returned from the East in the 13th century, he told of a frozen drink that consisted of a sweetened flower extract, paste or powder, which was diluted with water, then chilled with ice or snow. The drink was called *chorbet* in Turkish and *charab* in Persian, and it eventually evolved to become sorbet, or sherbet.

True frozen desserts were only made possible by the discovery that when ice and certain chemicals are combined, they form a liquid that is colder than the ice alone. One of the chemicals that works in this way is sodium chloride, or common salt. So when a mixture of ice and salt is packed around a container of a suitable liquid, the liquid in the container turns to ice.

As efficient ways of freezing were developed, the technique of making ices rapidly evolved into an art form and ices became a status symbol for the very rich. Soon banquet tables were glittering with beautiful ice pyramids. When Marie de' Medici married Henry IV of France in the late 16th century, she introduced the French court to *sorbetti*. Like sorbets enjoyed today, these were frequently eaten between main courses, but they differ from modern equivalents in that they were based on alcohol. Making these *sorbetti* was very skilled work, carried out by expert *liqueristes* such as Massialot, who featured recipes for chocolate ice and

ABOVE: *A coloured engraving showing fashionable ladies choosing ice cream, "An Embarrassment of Choices", from "Le Bon Genre", Paris 1827.*

MASSIALOT'S FROMAGE A L'ANGLOISE

"Take 16oz of sweet cream and the same of milk, 1/2lb powdered icing [confectioners'] sugar, stir in 3 egg yolks and boil it until it becomes a thin pap. Take it from the fire and pour it into your ice mould and put it on ice for 3 hours. When it is firm, withdraw the mould and warm it a little in order more easily to turn out your cheese, or else dip your mould for a moment in hot water, then serve in a compotier."

This recipe from Massialot's book The Court and Country Cook *was reprinted in Elizabeth David's book* Harvest of the Cold Months, *London, 1994.*

RIGHT: *A Sèvres dessert service was only for the very wealthy. It includes a* plat de ménage, *dish, cup and saucer and large ice cream bowl. From the Blue Cameo Service, Sèvres, 1778–9. Part of a collection belonging to the Hermitage, St Petersburg, Russia.*

custard ice in his cookbook published in 1692. Massailot referred to his ices as "cheeses", possibly because they were usually made in the dairy. Fruit flavours predominated in these early sorbets, but flower waters, including jasmine, violet, tuberose, orange blossom and jonquil, were also used, as were infusions of green fennel, burnet and chervil. Ices were usually served on exquisite china, often in epergnes or bowls made specifically for the purpose.

Britain was slow to follow this new European fashion. It was not until 1675 that we have the first recorded instance of ice cream being served, when King Charles II enjoyed strawberries and ice cream at a grand banquet. Interest in frozen desserts grew during the reign of William and Mary, and by the time Queen Anne ascended the throne in 1702, they were extremely popular in court circles.

In Regency Britain, elegance and extravagance were all-important, and London society was at the heart of the British Empire. During the reign of George III and later the Prince Regent, ice creams became even more fashionable. Frozen desserts were spectacular scented and shaped creations, set in complicated hinged moulds and served at grand balls, or brought to elaborate summer picnics in portable "ice caves" or cabinets.

Although these frozen desserts were very impressive to look at, they must have tasted rather gritty, as the ice crystals were not broken down by beating, nor was air introduced into the mixture.

EARLY RECIPES

Mary Eales, Confectioner to Queen Anne, was one of the first people to publish recipes for ice cream. Her book, *Mrs Eales's Receipts* (receipt being an early word for recipe), was published in 1718, some years after she supplied ice creams to the royal court. Her recipes call for very large amounts of ice to freeze these simple ice creams – as much as 10kg/20lb of ice mixed with 450g/1lb salt.

Mrs Eales' ice creams were frozen without the use of a churn, so would have tasted quite different from our modern ice creams. In 1722, a few years after Mary Eales published her book, Mary Smith included ten iced desserts in her publication *The Complete House-Keeper and Professional Cook*. These included Brown Bread Ice Cream, which is often considered a modern invention. Also on the list were Italian Ice Cream, Raspberry Cream, Orange Cream, Peach Cream and Apricot Cream.

Neither Mrs Eales' recipes nor those devised by Mary Smith contained eggs. Their inclusion was a later French refinement, which made ice cream considerably richer.

IMPROVEMENTS IN TASTE AND TEXTURE

A major advance that occurred in the 18th century was the discovery that beating ice cream until it was semi-frozen, then spooning it into a mould for a second freezing produced a much creamier and smoother result.

Flavourings became more adventurous at this time, and varied from exotic fruits such as bananas and pineapples to fresh berry fruit, preserves, chestnuts, cinnamon and white coffee cream. One of the more bizarre concoctions was a blend of lightly poached cucumber, ginger, brandy, coffee and cream. By 1885 books on making ice cream began to appear on the shelves, and cookery schools offered courses in making iced desserts.

THE ITALIAN CONNECTION

Italy had always been famous for its superior ice creams, but it was not until the late 19th century that Great Britain and the United States discovered the joy of Italian ice cream. This came about when political upheaval in Italy led to a huge exodus of young Italians, many of whom set up as ice cream makers in the countries that gave them refuge, often in makeshift premises on the dockside.

In the early days, ice cream street sellers were a cross between wandering musicians and street hawkers. Their organ music first attracted customers to their barrows, which ranged from quite simple, crude affairs to highly decorated and colourful carts. Some sellers even made early carts look like gondolas.

As ice cream grew in popularity, so the number of street sellers increased, and by the turn of the century, 900 ice cream barrows were registered in Clerkenwell, London, alone. Competition was fierce, and as more and more street traders arrived on the scene, fights between rivals became frequent as each vied for the best pitch or spot.

HYGIENE ISSUES

Much of the ice cream sold at the time was produced in slum conditions in domestic kitchens. Milk was boiled and left to stand overnight, then frozen with ice the next morning. The dishes in which the ice cream, known as penny licks, was served were reused, often without being washed. The inevitable outcome was that bacterial infections and diseases like tuberculosis spread rapidly. Following an attempt to ban the sale of ice cream, manufacturing moved to much more hygienic business premises, and barrows were licensed to sell ice cream only at designated points.

These actions helped to resolve the hygiene problem and restore peaceful trading. However, the event that did most to reinstate the reputation of ice cream sellers was the invention of the ice cream cone in the early 19th century. The ice cream could be scooped directly into the wafer cones, bowls became largely obsolete and food safety standards improved considerably.

Many more Italian immigrants came to Britain and America after the end of World War II in a bid to rebuild shattered lives and homes. Family-run cafes, ice cream parlours and ice cream factories were quickly set up by the immigrants, and Italian bakers lost no time in switching from cookie-making to producing ice cream cones and wafers to meet the demands dictated by the growing popularity of ice cream on the streets.

ABOVE LEFT: *As ice cream vendors prospered, some stalls became very elaborate, fixed structures.*

ABOVE AND LEFT: *Many early hand carts were replaced by horsedrawn carts, and these evolved into the ice cream vans used today.*

LARGE-SCALE PRODUCTION

The world's first ice cream plant was founded in the United States in 1851 by Jacob Fussell, a Baltimore milk dealer who wanted to find a new market for cream during the summer months, when the supply peaked. As a milk dealer, he had the advantage over his rivals and was able to undercut their prices. As a result, his ice cream became so successful that by 1864 he had opened factories in Washington, Boston and New York.

By the 1920s England was also producing ice cream on a grand scale. Two major market leaders soon emerged: Wall's and Lyons. Originally known for his meat pies, Thomas Wall embarked on ice cream manufacture as a way of boosting summer profits. At first, ice cream production was small, but Thomas's use of American production techniques paid off. As popularity and production grew, the company expanded from just one ice cream factory in the London suburb of Acton, with seven street sellers, in the 1920s, to 136 depots and 8,500 stop-me-and-buy-one tricycles by 1939. Also highly successful was the Lyons group, famous for its triple-flavoured Neapolitan ice cream and the Lyons Corner Houses in London.

REFRIGERATORS AND FREEZERS

Most bought ice cream at this time was consumed on the spot. Mechanical refrigerators had only been developed at the start of the 20th century, and early models were noisy and prohibitively expensive. However, as technology advanced, prices came down, although in Britain refrigerators remained a luxury item for the very rich until after World War II. It was not until the 1960s that refrigerators became commonplace, and it would take another decade before many households owned a domestic deep freezer, making it possible to store both bought and home-made ice cream.

CONES AND WAFERS

It was a young Italian immigrant to America, Italo Marchiony, who first came up with the idea of an edible container for ice cream. When he started selling his ice creams and sorbets on Wall Street in New York, he spooned them into glasses. These were cumbersome and wasteful, so he started making shaped cups from waffle batter. The cups proved very popular, and he patented them in 1902. Two years later, he patented an ice cream cone, although the credit for this innovation is often given to a Syrian, Ernest A. Hamwi. According to the story, Mr Hamwi was selling waffles at the World's Trade Fair in 1904 when a neighbouring ice cream

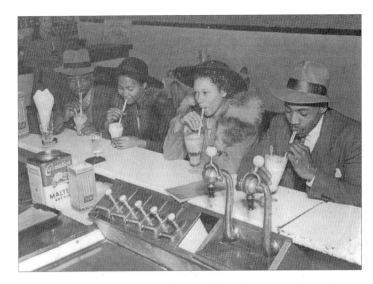

ABOVE: *An ice cream parlour, popular in the United States since Prohibition, when enterprising brewers converted their liquor bars to milk bars and served chilled ice cream sodas, thick creamy milk shakes and sundaes instead.*

ABOVE: *The one-penny wafer of the 1930s, and later the larger American ice cream cones, quickly grew in popularity with the young and the "young at heart".*

LEFT: *Lolly (popsicle) sticks at a French factory, 1963.*

seller sold out of dishes. He persuaded Mr Hamwi to roll one of his waffles into a cone, let it cool and filled it with his ice cream. Made with a mixture of flour, milk and sugar, the ice cream cone quickly became a favourite. To help prevent spills, a ring of non-crushable biscuit (cookie) was moulded to the top.

Other traders of the 1920s were reluctant to sell these large imported cones, as they were quite expensive and required a considerable amount of ice cream to fill them. They preferred to sell ice cream briquettes sandwiched between the much cheaper rectangular wafers. In the 1930s these wafers were so cheap that it was possible to sell ice creams for one penny. However, by 1935, waffles for ice cream were introduced to supersede wafers, with the rather unusual advertising slogan of "Have a waffle in the cinema". Sales of wafers continued until the 1950s, until soft serve ice cream cornets (cones) appeared on the scene and the famous "99" was introduced, complete with its much-loved chocolate flake bar.

THE ICE CREAM SUNDAE

In late 19th-century America, chemists (drugstores) throughout the country sold drinks that were based on soda water (seltzer). Flavoured with fruit syrups and whipped cream, sodas were popular with both young and old alike. In 1874, Robert Green of Philadelphia ran out of cream when making sodas for the 50th anniversary of the Franklin Institute. With a long queue of customers waiting to be served, he substituted ice cream, much to the delight of the guests.

The ice cream soda soon became very popular, but you couldn't buy one on a Sunday. This was because many people believed that the sodas were alcoholic, even though they were nothing of the kind, and indulging was regarded as improper, especially on Sundays. An ingenious drugstore concessionaire got around the ban by serving the ice cream and syrup without the soda (selzer). He called it Ice Cream Sunday. The name was later changed to Sundae, which was judged more seemly.

ABOVE: *A welcome refresher from the heat, ice cream is sold at an ice cream parlour near Broken Hill in New South Wales, Australia.*

ABOVE: *Although ice cream making started off slowly in Italy, it soon developed, and Italian ice creams have enjoyed worldwide popularity ever since.*

ICE CREAM PARLOURS

The first ice cream parlour is reputed to have been opened in New York City in 1776, although it wasn't until the Prohibition years of the 1920s that business really started to boom. Bar owners had always served ice cream during the hot summer months, and when Prohibition came in 1920, the more enterprising among them had the foresight to realize that swapping ice cream for hard liquor was one way of staying in business. By 1930, ice cream parlours had become very much a part of the American scene, and today there are ice cream parlours all over the world.

ICE CREAM MACHINES

Very early ice cream makers consisted of small earthenware or metal pots filled with milk or cream mixtures. These were then placed inside deep urns or cabinets lined with either wood or lead and surrounded with just ice, ice and straw, or ice and salt. The mixtures were then left to freeze. They must have been very hard and rather unpalatable by today's high standards, but such was their novelty value that they quickly became extremely popular with people of every age and social class.

ABOVE: *Despite the wintry weather, a young child enjoys ice cream near Winnipeg, Manitoba.*

George Washington, the first President of the United States, is said to have been so taken with ice cream when he was offered it in 1789 by Betsy Hamilton, wife of the Secretary to the Treasury, that he insisted that it be served regularly at official functions. Thomas Jefferson continued this presidential penchant for ice cream and even brought an ice cream maker back with him when he returned to the United States from a posting in France as Secretary of State.

By the middle of the 19th century, mechanized ice cream makers were introduced. These looked like wooden pails filled with an ice and salt mixture, and had a small metal canister inside for the ice cream.

HAND-CRANKED MACHINES

What really revolutionized the production of ice cream, however, was the hand-cranked ice cream machine. This kept the ice cream in continuous motion during freezing, preventing the formation of discernible ice crystals and introducing air. The most famous hand-cranked machine was invented in 1843 by Nancy Johnson, a naval officer's wife, in the United States. Later that century, in England, Agnes Marshall also developed a hand-cranked ice cream maker.

Traditional hand-cranked machines are handsome appliances. The outer casing is a tongue-and-groove wooden pail with a carrying handle. A stainless-steel ice cream container fits inside the tub, and the crank or turning handle powers the gear drive that turns the wooden dasher.

Operating the hand-cranked machine is simple, if tiring work. Having inserted the ice cream container into the pail, the dasher is fitted, and then chilled ice cream mixture is poured in. The lid is put on the container, the crank top is secured, and the space between the can and the pail is filled with a mixture of crushed ice and rock salt. After about five minutes, it is time to start churning.

With a manual machine, this means turning the crank continuously, slowly at first and then more rapidly, until the ice cream freezes and the crank becomes increasingly difficult to turn. At this point, water is drained from the machine, the top is lifted off and sufficient ice is cleared away to expose the top of the can. Ice cream on the dasher is scraped back into the can, and the dasher is removed. The ice cream can be eaten immediately, but purists prefer to repack it in the can, surrounding it with more ice, this time with a higher concentration of salt, and leave it to stand for 30 minutes to mature or "ripen".

The advantage of a hand-cranked ice cream machine is that very good ice cream can be made almost anywhere – on the porch, at a picnic – by anyone strong enough to turn the handle. Another plus is capacity. These machines make up to 6 litres/10 pints/6 quarts of ice cream in one sitting, which makes them ideal for entertaining. Perhaps these, plus their deliciously retro appearance, are among the reasons for their upsurge in popularity in America today. Electrically operated cranked machines are also available, mainly in the United States.

ABOVE: *With the introduction of mechanized ice churners, such as these wooden pails with metal canisters inside, ice cream could be produced and sold on a large scale by enterprising street sellers.*

FREEZER-AIDED MACHINES

As domestic refrigerators and freezers became more commonplace in people's homes, it was inevitable that someone would come up with the idea of an ice cream machine that could be operated inside the freezer. Several designs were pioneered in the early 1970s, including a simple rectangular stainless-steel box that was filled with a mixture of custard and cream and placed in the freezer cabinet of a refrigerator. The dashers or paddles were fitted on the underside of the lid. These turned constantly when the machine was connected to the electricity supply by means of a flattened flex, which enabled the door of the freezer to be closed while the ice cream maker was in operation. Some of these machines produced wonderfully smooth ice cream, but there were disadvantages. Most of them made only a small quantity and because the ice cream took a considerable amount of time to freeze, the motor was put under a lot of strain. The trailing flex was a hazard, and because the machine was out of sight during operation, the cook often failed to notice when the ice cream had frozen solid, causing paddles to snap and the motor to labour. Broken paddles and burnt-out motors contributed to the demise of this type of ice cream maker.

Making ice cream at home became a good deal simpler with the discovery that when a freezing solution was sealed within the walls of a container that was then frozen, the container became cold enough to freeze the ice cream mixture, even when operated at room temperature. The first machine to utilize this principle was invented in the 1980s. It resembled a traditional hand-cranked ice cream maker, but instead of a messy mixture of ice and salt, which needed to be replaced every time ice cream was made, the refrigerant was safely sealed inside the double-skinned bucket. The dasher that churned the ice cream had to be turned by hand every few minutes, but the machine didn't require the same amount of elbow grease as classic hand-cranked versions and was much more time- and energy-efficient.

LEFT: *Illustration of an early ice cream machine using a hand-cranking device for churning the ice cream.*

ABOVE: *Commercial machines, like those used in this ice cream factory in Holstich, Germany in 1895, were the forerunners of modern ice cream makers.*

The next stage was to produce an ice cream maker that operated on the same principle, but in which the mixture could be churned automatically during freezing. The bucket was pre-frozen and then removed from the freezer. A lid that incorporated the dasher and motor was fitted on top, the machine was plugged in and switched on, and the ice cream mixture was poured in. The ice cream was then frozen relatively quickly, and the dasher continued to turn until the thickening mixture caused it to become sluggish, which signalled that the ice cream was ready to be decanted and eaten.

Such machines remain the mainstay of the lower end of the market today. They come in various shapes and sizes, some with tall, bulbous ice cream tubs; others looking more like cake tins (pans). In some cases, the container that goes into the freezer is the base of the machine, merely requiring a dasher and motor to be fitted to it after it has been frozen. In other models, the bucket is separate, and must be fitted into an outer casing once the refrigerant is frozen. The advantage of the former machine is that if you store it permanently in the freezer, as suggested by the manufacturer, then it is ready to be used at all times, and the only part that should be housed in a kitchen cupboard is the lid, with its motor and dasher. The type of machine that has a separate bucket is not ready for immediate use and takes up more storage space in the kitchen, but tends to be easier to assemble.

Freezer-aided machines take around 30–45 minutes to make ice cream. It is important that the dasher is rotating when the ice cream mixture is poured in (usually through an aperture in the lid) so that churning begins immediately and the dasher continues to move smoothly. If the cream or custard mixture is poured in before the dasher has been started, the mixture may freeze on contact with the sides or base of the bucket, preventing the dasher from turning easily, causing wear to the motor and preventing the production of perfect ice cream.

One of the latest machines to arrive on the UK market is the soft serve ice cream maker. Like the seaside treat that gave the machine its name, it includes a dispenser, so the ice cream comes out rather like toothpaste from a tube, and can be easily swirled into a dish or cone. Quite a lot air is incorporated during the mixing and freezing process, so the ice cream is lighter and airier than the dense, rich ice cream produced by conventional machines.

MAKING ICE CREAM AT HOME

With the increased availability of affordable ingredients and improvements to ice cream makers, middle-class housewives sought the advice of highly skilled cooks, such as Mrs Agnes B. Marshall and Mrs Beeton. In 1885 Agnes Marshall published her first book, in which she included detailed advice on making a range of ice creams, such as "cheap", "ordinary" and "common" ice cream. Her "cheap ice cream" was made using 1 pint (600ml|2½ cups) of cream, 8 egg yolks and ¼lb (115g|4oz|½ cup) of sugar. Next came her "ordinary ice cream", in which the cream was replaced with milk. Her "common ice cream" was made with the same quantity of milk and sugar, but only two whisked eggs, while the "ordinary ice cream" dispensed with eggs altogether, and thickened the sweetened milk with arrowroot (15g|½oz|2 tbsp).

ABOVE: *An ice cream mould.*

RIGHT: *An early hand-cranked ice cream machine.*

RIGHT: *Illustration from* Süsse Speisen und Eisbomben, *published in Germany in 1907, showing a variety of iced confections.*

The soft serve machine is great fun for families with small children and could well become the main attraction at birthday parties. However, the machine is quite difficult to assemble and does have its limitations. It makes delicious ice cream, but it is not suitable for mixtures containing chunky ingredients, such as nuts, pieces of fruit or chocolate chips. It is recommended that only soft-serve recipes supplied with the machine be used, and these tend to be quite basic. Should hard ice cream be required, the soft-serve can be spooned into a tub and placed in the freezer until solid.

All of these machines are affordable and easy to operate, but because they depend on a period of pre-freezing of the tub, you can't make ice cream on impulse. If you have enough freezer space to keep the bucket or tub permanently frozen, as the manufacturers recommend, some spontaneity is possible, but you still won't be able to make successive batches of ice cream without a spare tub.

FREESTANDING MACHINES

If you really love ice cream – and make it often – it is worth investing in a top-of-the-range freestanding machine. These are worktop versions of the huge machines used in ice cream factories, and each has a built-in compressor. Pre-chilling is still necessary, but this only takes ten minutes at most, after which time the dasher is turned on and the ice cream mixture is poured in.

The three main advantages of this type of machine are convenience, speed and excellent texture. Use good quality ingredients, and the ice cream they produce will be virtually perfect, but you'll need to produce a lot of it to justify the price of the appliance. Another factor to consider is size. One of these, a food processor and a kettle and your working area will be severely restricted. Also these machines tend to be noisier than freezer-chilled types, so if you are trying to make a batch of Chunky Chocolate Ice Cream or Rocky Road Ice Cream without attracting the attention of the children, you may be rumbled.

Whatever type of machine you buy, making ice cream will be a great deal easier than the old-fashioned method of chilling in a shallow pan and beating it by hand at regular intervals during the freezing process. With the minimum of effort, you'll be able to transform top quality ingredients into a delectable iced dessert.

THE RISE OF THE ICE CREAM GIANTS

In the early 1930s a young man by the name of Reuben Mattus was often to be found on the streets of the Bronx in New York, selling his mother's home-made ice cream from a horse and buggy.

BELOW: *This traditional churn has been modified with the addition of an electric crank. These retro churns produce large amounts of ice cream and are very popular.*

ABOVE: *A traditional hand-cranked ice cream machine. The metal turning handle powers the gear drive and turns the wooden dasher.*

The family business prospered in the years that followed, and in 1961 Reuben launched a new product, a superior, richly flavoured ice cream containing butterfat, which did not incorporate very much air, producing a dense texture. He called it Häagen-Dazs. At first there were just three basic flavours – chocolate, vanilla and coffee – but the ice cream's fans soon demanded more, and the delis that stocked it found it difficult to keep up with demand.

In 1973 the first Häagen-Dazs shop was opened, and ten years later Mr Mattas sold out to the Pillsbury Company. Today Häagen-Dazs remains a world leader, with flavours such as blueberry cheesecake, chocolate cheesecake and macadamia brittle.

Five years before Mr Mattas sold his business, two young American college friends, Ben Cohen and Jerry Greenfield, began making ice cream in a renovated petrol (gas) station in Burlington, Vermont. They bought an old-fashioned hand-cranked machine, did an ice-cream-making course by correspondence and, after considerable experimentation, went into business. Sales soon rocketed and Ben & Jerry's ice cream is now sold all over the world.

ICE CREAM TODAY

Ice cream is one of the world's favourite foods, enjoyed in all countries and in all seasons. The countries with the highest rate of consumption include the United States, New Zealand and Australia. Sales in Japan are rising rapidly, and even in cooler countries such as Denmark and Finland, ice cream is extremely popular. Although more ice cream is sold in the summer than in the winter, it is bought, eaten and enjoyed all year round. In Russia, for instance, ice cream can be bought from street kiosks even when the ground is covered in deep snow.

It is now possible to buy luxury ice creams in a vast array of flavours from supermarkets, delis and ice cream parlours, but indulgence often comes at a price, and many individuals prefer to make their own ice cream at home, especially now that efficient and relatively inexpensive machines are readily available.

making
ice cream

Creating delicious ice cream at home is surprisingly simple, requires little equipment and is enormously satisfying. Covering every aspect of making ices in all of their variety, as well as sauces, cones, baskets and decorations, this chapter provides the skills and techniques necessary for even the most ambitious iced desserts.

Ice cream machines

Ice cream can be made by hand, but it is a time-consuming and laborious process. An ice cream maker produces excellent iced desserts, including low-fat ice cream and sorbets, with very little effort. There are a number of models on the market, priced to suit all pockets and to meet all requirements.

There are basically two types of ice cream maker on the market: freezer assisted machines, and machines that have their own compressors which do not need to go in the freezer.

FREEZER ASSISTED MACHINES

These machines are usually cheaper than machines with their own compressors, and there are many different models available, which perform in different ways.

Simple ice cream machines

The cheapest option is a simple machine that consists of a double-skinned bowl and a separate motor unit. Between the walls of the bowl is liquid refrigerant. When frozen solid – a process that can take up to 24 hours – the bowl becomes super-cooled, and when the dasher or beater and motor are fitted, the mixture to be churned is

BELOW: *This simple freezer assisted machine is easy to use and relatively inexpensive.*

rapidly transformed into ice cream or sorbet. The drawback with this type of machine is that it requires forward planning in order to freeze the bowl for 24 hours – unless you have enough room to keep the bowl permanently in the freezer – and the capacity is limited. Some of the machines are quite awkward to assemble, and because the aperture where the mixture is poured in is relatively small, spills are commonplace. You can't make successive batches of ice cream unless you have a spare frozen bowl, but that shouldn't prove a problem unless you are a serial ice cream eater! For the average family for whom ice cream is a regular but not daily dessert, this type of machine is ideal.

Quick ice cream machines

One type, which performs very well, only takes half an hour to make a batch of ice cream. The double-skinned bowl is lifted out of the casing and wrapped in a plastic bag before being frozen. When the refrigerant has cooled

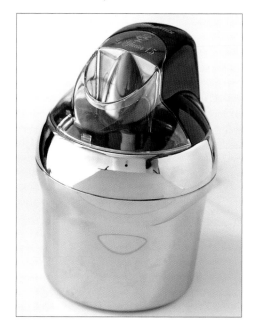

ABOVE: *This compact freezer assisted model comes in both white and modern chrome finishes.*

sufficiently, the bowl is replaced and the lid, with the dasher, is fitted on top. The motor is turned on, and the mixture is poured in through the lid. The advantages of this machine are ease of assembly and operation, a quiet motor and a bowl with a large surface area for easy scooping. The drawback is that it requires quite a bit of storage space.

Quick churn ice cream machines

Other freezer assisted machines are available on the market with fewer parts, in which the ice-bucket-shaped bowl itself forms the base of the machine. Once it is fully frozen – which can take some time – all you need to do is fit the lid with the dasher and motor, switch it on and pour in the ice cream mixture to be churned. If you keep the bowl permanently in the freezer, it will be ready to use at all times and the remaining parts will take up little room in your kitchen cupboard. This type of model tends to come in two sizes, one delivering 650ml|1 pint 2fl oz|2⅔ cups of ice cream and the larger 900ml|1½ pints|3¾ cups. On the negative side, the motor is quite loud and fitting the lid can be difficult.

Soft serve ice cream machines

A third type of machine, and one that can be quite fun for the child in the family or even the child in you, is a soft serve maker. This type of machine dispenses soft serve ice cream in swirls and whirls, so you can make ices just like the ones sold at the seaside. The soft serve ice cream machine comes with four separate nozzles and is relatively easy to operate, although assembling the machine and cleaning it can be awkward. It is also very loud, so there's no question of making a sundae in secret, and it is not suitable for mixtures containing any chunks, such as nuts or chocolate chips or fruit.

BUILT-IN COMPRESSOR MACHINES

If you can afford it, and have plenty of space on your counter-top, consider buying an ice cream maker with a built in freezer unit or compressor. These machines are ready for use ten minutes after activating the compressor, and produce very good ice cream with ease. Most have both a fixed bowl, and a smaller bucket for quantities up to 600ml|1 pint. To make successive batches of ice cream, you can use the bucket first, then lift it out and make a second lot of ice cream in the larger bowl.

ABOVE: *The soft serve ice cream maker is one of the latest types of machine available.*

The real advantage of a machine with its own freezing unit, or compressor, is that it needs only 5–10 minutes' pre-chilling before the dasher motor is switched on and the liquid is added. The major drawback is cleaning the machine, since the fixed bowl cannot be lifted out, nor should the machine be tilted. After scooping out the ice cream, the bowl must be washed thoroughly with a sponge filled with hot soapy water, then rinsed with cold water before being dried with kitchen paper. If you use the smaller bowl, you will avoid this chore, but will still need to wipe up the alcohol that must be used between the two bowls to conduct the cold.

Some models have the dasher motor inside the machine, so the operation is smooth and efficient. This type of machine is easy to use

ABOVE: *This handsome counter-top model has its own built-in compressor for creating luxury ice cream.*

but does take up a lot of space. It should not be tipped or tilted (the refrigerant must settle before use), so it is best kept permanently on the worktop.

THE FREEZER

An efficient freezer is essential for pre-chilling bowls or buckets for basic ice cream makers, and for storing the ice cream once you have made it. For making ice cream the temperature should be –18ºC|–66ºF. A freezer thermometer is a useful tool. The colder the freezer the more quickly the ice will freeze, resulting in smaller ice crystals and smoother ice cream.

BELOW: *This freestanding machine incorporates an internal dasher motor.*

QUESTIONS TO ASK WHEN BUYING

• Is the machine virtually ready to go or does it require lengthy pre-freezing?

• If the bowl needs to be pre-frozen, which shape will fit your freezer best?

• How much storage space does the machine require? Remember that a machine with its own compressor is best kept on the worktop.

• How noisy is the motor? (Ask to see – or hear – the machine in operation before you buy, if possible.)

• What is the maximum – and minimum – capacity of the machine?

• Is it possible to make successive batches of ice cream?

• How easy is it to assemble and take apart the machine for cleaning?

• Is there a decent-size aperture for pouring in the mixture to be churned?

• Can you buy extra bowls for pre-freezing?

Basic equipment

You will probably already have most of the peripheral equipment required for making ice creams, or can adapt existing kitchen equipment. Spoons can double as scoops, bowls can be used as moulds, and plastic boxes with tight-fitting lids are ideal for storage. Some specialist items are useful, however.

SCOOPS, SPOONS AND SCRAPERS

There are plenty of ice cream scoops on the market. Choose from half-moon-shaped stainless-steel scoops with sleek steel handles, simple spoon-shaped scoops with metal handles or easy-grip moulded plastic handles, or brightly coloured plastic scoops with quick release levers. Among the most efficient scoops are those with antifreeze solution embedded in the handle. This is activated by the warmth of your hand, and enables the ice cream to slide effortlessly off the scoop.

When scooping ice cream out of a tub or box, do not dig deep: the trick is to draw the scoop smoothly across the surface of the ice cream so that a natural ball-shape is formed. Some people recommend dipping the scoop in water between uses, but this is not a good idea as the water will freeze on contact, spoiling the texture of the ice cream. For tiny balls of ice cream, use melon ballers. Arrange the scoops on a plate so that they resemble a bunch of grapes, or pile them up.

Use only plastic or rubber spoons and scrapers for removing ice cream from the buckets or bowls of ice cream makers, as scratching the containers will impair their efficiency and could trap germs.

MOULDS

Although you can buy bombe, dariole and ring moulds designed specifically for ice cream, such items can be costly and take up valuable space

ABOVE: *Specialized bombe, dariole and ring moulds will ensure a professional finish, but they can be expensive pieces of kitchen equipment.*

LEFT: *Individual metal steamed pudding moulds can be used if lined with clear film.*

in the kitchen. Improvise by using different size mixing bowls, cake tins (pans) and individual steamed pudding moulds. Line them with several layers of clear film (plastic wrap) first, using a generous amount of wrapping so that there is enough overlap to cover the entire exposed surface of the ice cream to prevent it from drying out in the freezer.

EVERYDAY EQUIPMENT

To make rectangular ice cream bombes or terrines, you can use metal loaf tins (pans). Unless they have a non-stick finish, line them with clear film. Tins that have sloping sides can be adapted. Simply cut a piece of cardboard the length and height of the tin and use it to alter the shape of the tin. Line with clear film, pushing it carefully into the corners.

For bombes or cassatas you can use a plastic bowl with a lid. These make ideal ice cream moulds, as the thin plastic conducts the cold well in the freezer, and the dessert can be easily turned out by by running the bowl under a hot tap and then flexing the plastic.

ABOVE: *Use melon ballers to make miniature scoops of ice cream and sorbet, and pile them up on a plate.*

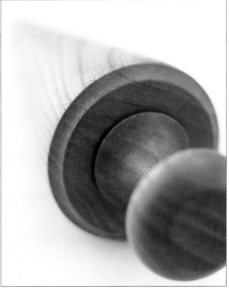

ABOVE: *This wooden cone mould is a very simple but useful tool for making professional-looking cones.*

ABOVE: *Unmoulding kulfi is easy with a specially designed all-in-one kulfi mould.*

Instead of buying special moulds for kulfi, use conical lolly (popsicle) moulds or new disposable plastic cups, which work almost as well. For individual moulds, line old china cups, metal dariole moulds or individual metal steamed pudding moulds with several layers of clear film, which makes it easier to turn out the frozen dessert. If you can lay your hands on them, the tiny plastic pots with lids used for freezing baby food are ideal.

BELOW: *Ice cream scoops are available in many different shapes, materials and colours.*

STORAGE BOXES

For storage, you will need a selection of freezerproof containers in varying sizes, with tightly fitting lids to eliminate the transfer of strong smells and flavours and prevent the surface of the ice cream from drying out. Good quality bought ice cream tubs and air-tight sandwich boxes are ideal. Placing a piece of clear film on the surface of the ice cream is a sensible additional precaution, preventing frost build-up and preventing the surface from becoming dry. Try to keep the ice cream away from strongly flavoured products in the freezer.

TURNING OUT A FROZEN BOMBE

To unmould an iced dessert in a metal or plastic mould, dip it in hot, but not boiling, water, leave for a few seconds, then blot the excess water. If the mould is lined with clear film, carefully insert a knife between the film and the mould to loosen the ice cream. Invert the mould on a serving plate, lift off the mould and peel away the film.

If the mould is made of glass or china, do not dip it in hot water, or it may break. Instead, invert the basin on a serving plate, then warm the outside by covering it with a hot dish towel. Count to 20 and then lift the basin off.

When dipping moulds, use hot tap water rather than boiling water from the kettle, which would cause the outside of the ice cream to melt instantly and run over the plate when turned out. Boiling water would also be dangerous, as it could splash.

Basic ingredients

Nothing beats the cool, creamy smoothness of the ultimate indulgence, home-made ice cream. The choice of flavours and flavour combinations is limited only by your own imagination, so begin with our basic recipes and adapt or develop them to incorporate all the tastes you love. You will rapidly build a repertoire of wonderful iced desserts, all completely additive-free and made with only the ingredients that you choose to include.

Ice cream

Cream

You just couldn't make true ice cream without lashings of cream. Surprisingly, whipping cream, with its natural creamy taste, makes the best ice cream, especially when mixed with strong rich flavours such as coffee, toffee or chocolate. Double (heavy) cream is, however, a must for vanilla or Brown Bread Ice Cream. Clotted cream and crème fraîche, the thick, rich lightly soured French-style cream, make delicious additions to fruit, honey and spice ice creams. Do be careful when using double or clotted cream as their high butter-fat content can give the ice cream a buttery flavour and texture, especially if it is overchurned. Avoid UHT creams as the flavour is too strong.

ABOVE: *Freshly laid eggs and double or whipping cream gives home-made ice cream its luxury flavour.*

Milk

There is a wide choice of milk in most supermarkets – from skimmed, semi-skimmed (low-fat), full-fat (whole) and breakfast milk, to the now more readily available goat's milk and soya milk. Skimmed milk is best avoided when making ice cream at home, due to its low fat content and "thin" taste, but it is difficult to distinguish between semi-skimmed and full-fat milk, especially when mixed with cream. Full-fat, semi-skimmed and goat's milk all make delicious ice cream.

Yogurt

The choice of yogurt is highly personal: it seems people either love ice cream that contains yogurt, or absolutely hate it! If you are not sure how your family will react to it, start with the mild bio-style natural (plain) yogurt, with its creamy smoothness, and, if that is successful, work up to using the stronger, sharper sheep's and goat's milk yogurts.

Cheese

Light, virtually fat-free fromage frais can be added to fruit or vanilla ice creams and is ideal for those who adore ice cream but have to watch their fat intake. Ricotta, an Italian whey cheese, has a white, creamy, soft texture. It is similar to a cross between cottage and cream cheese and can be used successfully in certain ice creams. For the richest results of all, try mascarpone, another Italian cheese. It has a deep buttery-yellow colour and a texture similar to that of cream cheese. For the best of both worlds, mix mascarpone with fromage frais for a rich-tasting, reduced-fat dessert.

Non-dairy products

Look out for soya milk, either unsweetened or sweetened, in long-life cartons, and canned coconut milk – both ideal for vegans or those on a milk-free diet. Coconut milk is also a great standby for a dinner-party ice cream when mixed with lime or lemon.

Eggs

Where possible use freshly laid, organic eggs for the best colour and flavour. They cost a little more than ordinary eggs but make a great difference to the finished result of home-made ice cream.

ABOVE: *Muscovado sugar can be a delicious sweetener.*

Sweeteners

Caster (superfine) sugar has been used in most of the recipes, as its fine crystals dissolve quickly in the custard, maintaining a smooth, silky texture. Granulated (white) sugar is used for making nut brittle (praline), a delicious ingredient in some of the speciality ices. Muscovado (molasses) and light muscovado (brown) sugar can also be used as a sweetener in some recipes, where the darker colour and stronger flavour is used to great effect. Honey and maple syrup also make delicious additions, either on their own or mixed with caster sugar. They are particularly good in ice cream flavoured with nuts.

Cornflour

Purists will throw up their hands in horror at the idea of cornflour (cornstarch) being used in the custard for an ice cream. They might well argue that it is far better to make the custard in a double boiler or a large heatproof bowl set over simmering water. It is certainly true that cornflour is not a standard ingredient in a classic custard, but it does help to stabilize the custard and reduces the risk of curdling. Custard that contains a little cornflour is easier to handle, so can be gently cooked in a heavy pan. It will thicken in 4–5 minutes, whereas it would take 15 minutes or more in a double boiler, thus greatly reducing the cooking time.

COOK'S TIP *Put leftover egg whites in a small plastic box. Cover with a tight-fitting lid and label the box clearly. Freeze up to 6 months and thaw at room temperature for 4 hours. Use to make pavlovas, sorbets, meringues and meringue-based ice creams.*

Water ices

Sugar syrup

A simple sugar syrup is made by heating a mixture of caster sugar and water in a medium pan, stirring until the sugar has dissolved. It is no longer thought essential to boil the syrup, just to heat it for long enough to dissolve the sugar. Caster sugar has been used for syrups in the recipe section of this book because it dissolves very rapidly, but granulated sugar can also be used, as can light muscovado sugar or honey. Once made and cooled, the syrup can be stored in the refrigerator for several days.

Flavouring

You can choose from a wide range of flavourings, including fresh fruit purées such as strawberry, raspberry, peach or pineapple, or a mixture of these with some of the more exotic fruits such as passion fruit, mango and lime. Dried fruits can be steeped in apple or grape juice or in water and brandy or a liqueur mixture before being puréed and added to the custard mixture. Citrus rinds (orange, lemon or lime) can be infused in the hot syrup for extra flavour and then fresh juice can be added to heighten and strengthen the flavour. Spice infusions or mixtures of spices and fruits also work very well and create unusual ices that are particularly successful with people who prefer a light dessert that is not too sweet or rich.

ABOVE: *Honey can be used on its own or with sugar.*

Egg white

The purpose of adding egg white to a semi-frozen sorbet is twofold. First, it helps to stabilize the mixture, which is important for those sorbets that melt quickly, and second, it can be used to lighten very dense or fibrous sorbets, such as those made from blackcurrants or blackberries. The egg white requires only the minimum of beating with a fork to loosen it and need not be whisked until frothy or standing in peaks as previously thought.

HOW TO SEPARATE AN EGG

Crack the egg on the side of a bowl. Gently ease the halves apart, keeping the yolk in one half and letting the white fall into the bowl below. Separate any remaining egg white from the yolk by swapping the yolk from one shell half to the other. Do this several times if necessary, until all the egg white has fallen into the bowl and what remains is the pure egg yolk. If you do drop any egg yolk into the bowl below, scoop it out with one of the eggshell halves; the jagged edges will trap the yolk and prevent it from sliding back into the bowl.

Flavourings

Visit a modern ice cream parlour and you'll be dazzled by the number of flavours available. But there is no comparison to the endless possibilities you can create at home. Spices, herbs, fruits of every kind, flower waters, chocolate, coffee and nuts can all be used – singly or in combination. Experiment to find the tastes you and your family like best, remembering that freezing dulls some flavours, so you can often afford to be bold.

Herbs and flowers

Edible flowers

A sprinkling of just a few delicate, colourful petals or tiny flower heads from the garden can turn even a few simple scoops of home-made strawberry or vanilla ice cream into an elegant dinner-party dessert.

A few vibrant pansies or tiny violas mixed with primrose petals or even a few dainty violets would be perfect for a springtime party, while pastel-coloured rose petals, borage flowers or sprigs of lavender would make a fine decoration in summer, as would a misty haze of elderflowers or sweet cicely flowers.

For something bolder, use nasturtiums or yellow or orange marigold petals (*Calendula*), but not French or African marigolds. If selecting other flowers, please be aware that not all flowers are edible. Avoid plants that grow from a bulb or that would not be found in a herb garden, as these may at worst be poisonous or at best have a very unpleasant flavour.

Flower waters

Orange flower or orange blossom water and rose water add a delicate fragrance to ground almond or summer berry ice creams and sorbets. Add a few drops and seal the bottle well to prevent evaporation.

Herbs

Rosemary, bay, mint and lavender make wonderful additions to creamy ice creams, sherbets or sorbets. For best results infuse a few sprigs of rosemary or lavender, two to three whole bay leaves or a small bunch of fresh mint in cream or sugar syrup that has just come to the boil. Leave in the liquid until cool, then strain. You can also add a little fresh chopped mint or other extra herbs to the finished ice cream or sorbet.

RIGHT: *Sprigs of flowers or flower water give a delicate flavour to ice creams and sorbets.*

Spices

Ginger

TYPES/FORMS: The rhizome of an elegant tropical plant, ginger appears in many guises. The root is widely available fresh and is also preserved in sugar syrup as stem ginger. Chopped candied ginger and crystallized ginger are other forms of this delicious spice.

USES: Ginger makes a wonderful ice cream ingredient just on its own, but it gives a glorious lift to fruit ices, especially with fruit such as rhubarb or pears, and it is a natural partner for tropical fruit. Preserved ginger, ginger syrup and ginger wine make delicious ice cream sauces.

PREPARATION: Peel root ginger, then slice or chop it thinly. Alternatively, grate it with the fine-toothed surface of a grater. Slice or chop preserved stem ginger; finely chop candied or crystallized ginger if pieces are large.

Using ginger

1 Peel away the skin on the ginger root, using a swivel-blade vegetable peeler or a small, sharp knife. Take care when peeling to remove only the thin outer skin.

2 Grate the ginger on the fine section of a regular grater or a nutmeg grater. This is easiest to do if the ginger is frozen. It will thaw instantly on being grated.

Vanilla

TYPES/FORMS: Seed pods of the climbing vanilla orchid plant are sold singly or in pairs. The spice is also finely ground, mixed with sugar and sold in sachets labelled vanilla sugar. It is best known, however, as vanilla essence (extract).

The pods are picked while still unripe. On drying, their yellow colour deepens to a dark brown and they acquire a natural coating of vanillin crystals, which are the source of the characteristic spicy aroma. The word "vanilla" comes from the Spanish *vainilla*, meaning "little sheath". Although always associated with sweet dishes, the vanilla pod is not itself sweet.

Beware of cheap vanilla flavourings as their harsh, almost bitter, flavour can be overpowering and could spoil the delicate flavour of some ice creams. The better quality vanilla essence is always labelled "natural vanilla essence".

USES: Vanilla is delicious in ice cream, whipped cream and custard and is used extensively when making patissiere cream and confectionery.

PREPARATION: Slit the whole vanilla pod, add it to cream or milk that has just come to the boil, then leave to cool and infuse. Lift up the pod, and holding it over the liquid, scrape the tiny black seeds with a small knife so that they fall into the liquid. The flavoured cream or milk makes excellent ice cream. Don't throw pods away after use. Rinse, pat dry with kitchen paper and store two or three in a jar of caster (superfine) sugar to make your own vanilla sugar. Vanilla essence is highly concentrated, and you only need 2.5–5ml/½–1 tsp for ice cream.

Cinnamon

TYPES/FORMS: Cinnamon is obtained from the bark of the cinnamon tree, which is native to India. The bark is rolled into sticks or quills and dried. Cinnamon is also sold finely ground. The ground spice is seldom used in ice creams, except as a decoration, although it is widely used in baking. Cassia is a related spice. It resembles cinnamon in terms of aroma and flavour but is coarser and more pungent. Cassia is usually cheaper than cinnamon.

USES: Ice cream may not be the obvious use for cinnamon, a spice better known as an ingredient in cakes, biscuits and savoury dishes, but it adds a delicious flavour, especially with fruits such as peaches or nectarines.

PREPARATION: Infuse halved cinnamon sticks in milk or cream that has just come to the boil. Continue to simmer for 5–10 minutes until the cinnamon has imparted its flavour to the liquid, strain the milk or cream and use it to make custard as the basis for ice cream. Cinnamon sticks can also be used to flavour fruit purées or compotes by infusing in the liquid in the same way.

Using vanilla

Using a sharp knife, slit a whole vanilla pod. Add it to milk or cream that has just come to the boil. For maximum flavour, scrape out the tiny black seeds from the pod and let them fall into the milk or cream.

Nutmeg

TYPES/FORMS: Sold whole, nutmegs are the dried seeds of the fruit of the nutmeg tree, which is native to the tropics. Blades of mace, the pretty orange outer coating, are also sold separately, and both are sold ground.

USES: Nutmeg's wonderfully aromatic and slightly bitter flavour complements both sweet and savoury dishes. It is delicious in milk-based desserts such as ice cream.

PREPARATION: For the best flavour, grate a little off a whole nutmeg as and when you need it, using the fine-toothed surface of a grater or, better still, a small nutmeg grater. Ready-ground nutmeg tends to rapidly lose its pungency when it is stored.

Cloves

TYPES/FORMS: The unopened flower buds of a tree related to the myrtle, cloves look like tiny nails. They are available whole and ground.

USES: Although cloves are most commonly used in savoury dishes, they are also widely used in desserts, particularly with apples and other fruits. Their pungent flavour means that they are a somewhat unlikely ingredient in ice cream, but if used sparingly, they add an intriguing flavour.

PREPARATION: Infuse whole cloves in milk or cream. This is especially appropriate when making a custard to form the basis of a fruit ice cream. Don't overdo this flavouring – the taste should be subtle and not strident.

Star anise

These pretty star-shaped pods are a favourite of Chinese cooks, but are becoming popular in the West. Use them whole for sauces and compotes, or infuse them in sugar syrups or custards for ices with a lovely aniseed flavour.

Using cardamom

If the recipe calls for cardamom seeds, crush the pods with the back of a cook's knife until they split. If necessary, use the tip of the knife to remove any remaining seeds from the pods. Use both the pod and the seeds for maximum flavour.

Cardamom

Traditionally used in Indian, Arabian and North African cooking, cardamom also adds a wonderful delicate aromatic fragrance to sorbets, ice creams and fruit compotes.

Lemon grass

Mainly known for the delicate lemon fragrance it contributes to Thai and Vietnamese cookery, lemon grass is now widely available. Most supermarkets stock the fresh stems, which are pale green and tipped with white; it is also available as dried whole stems or ground lemon grass and sold in jars. To extract the delicate flavour the dried stems must be soaked in warm water for at least two hours before use. Fresh lemon grass can be finely sliced or crushed and infused in the milk to be used for custard-based ice cream or infused in the sugar syrup for a granita or sorbet.

BELOW: *Star anise, vanilla pods, cinnamon sticks and ground ginger all add subtle flavours to ice creams.*

Chocolate

Choosing the best

A chocolate with a good, strong flavour is vital when making ice creams as the flavour of the chocolate is dulled when it is mixed with custard and cream. For the best and strongest flavour choose a good quality dark or bitter chocolate with a high proportion of cocoa solids. Confectioners and good food shops will have a selection of superior chocolates, but many of the larger supermarkets now stock several different types of good quality cooking chocolate. Choose one with "luxury" or "Belgian" on the label as it will almost certainly have at least 75 per cent cocoa solids, and good flavour and taste will be guaranteed.

Chocolate Menier can also be used. It has a stronger flavour and is less sweet than some other types of chocolate, but is well suited to ice cream making. Plain (semisweet) dessert chocolate contains between 30 and 60 per cent cocoa solids. Check the side of the pack for details – the higher the cocoa solids, the stronger the chocolate flavour will be, so avoid using any chocolate with less than 45 per cent cocoa solids if possible.

In general, chocolate cake coverings should be avoided, as these have a mild, less chocolatey taste. With their added vegetable fat, they are more suited to making chocolate curls or caraque. What you can do, however, is to mix equal amounts of cake covering and luxury dark (bittersweet) chocolate. This way, you get the easy melting and moulding qualities of the former, plus the superior taste of the latter.

How to melt chocolate

Couverture

This pure chocolate contains no fats other than cocoa butter, and has a high sheen and a creamy texture. Couverture is used mainly by professionals, and is normally only available from specialist suppliers. It generally requires "tempering" before use in order to distribute the cocoa fat evenly and give the desired result. This is quite a lengthy process that involves warming and working the chocolate until it reaches 32°C|90°F. Couverture is usually used for moulding or decorating because of its glossy finish. It is available as white, milk and dark chocolate drops or as a block.

White chocolate

As when buying dark chocolate, choose "luxury" white chocolate or "Swiss" white chocolate for the best flavour. White chocolate is made from cocoa butter extracted during the production of cocoa solids. Although it includes about 2 per cent cocoa solids, many purists would argue that this is not nearly enough to make it a true chocolate, especially as the cocoa butter is then mixed with milk solids, sugar and flavourings.

As a result of these additional ingredients, white chocolate does require extra care when being melted: it quickly hardens if overheated. Do check the pack before buying, and choose a brand with a minimum of 25 per cent cocoa butter, as any chocolate with less than this will be difficult to melt. The more cocoa butter there is, the creamier and softer the chocolate will be. Some brands may even include vegetable fat or oils, so always check the ingredients list.

Melting chocolate in a microwave

Break dark or milk chocolate into equal-sized small squares, and place them in a bowl that can be safely used in a microwave. Heat it on full power, allowing 2 minutes for 115g|4oz chocolate and 3 minutes for 200g|7oz. The chocolate will retain its shape until you stir it. Don't be tempted to heat it for longer as you may cause the chocolate to "seize", which spoils the chocolate and causes it to clump and harden. White chocolate melts easily and is best microwaved on medium power or in a bowl placed over a pan of just boiled water.

1 Pour water into a pan until it is about one third full. Bring to the boil, switch off the heat, then fit a heatproof bowl over the pan, making sure that the water does not touch the base of the bowl. Break the chocolate into equal-size small pieces and put it in the bowl.

2 Leave the chocolate pieces for 4–5 minutes, without stirring, until the chocolate has melted – the chocolate pieces will hold their shape. Stir the chocolate briefly until it is smooth, before folding it into ice cream, or using it as the basis of a sauce.

Cocoa

This rich, strong, dark powder is made by extracting some of the cocoa butter during chocolate production. What remains is a block containing around 20 per cent cocoa butter, although this percentage varies with each manufacturer. The cocoa is then ground and mixed with sugar and starch. The addition of starch means that cocoa must be cooked briefly to remove the raw, floury taste. This can be done by mixing it to a paste with a little boiling water, which is the usual technique when flavouring ice cream. If the cocoa is to be used in a sauce, it will probably be mixed with hot milk.

The very best cocoa is produced in Holland. It is alkalized, a process that removes the acidity and produces a cocoa with a mellow, well-rounded flavour. The technique was devised by the manufacturer Van Houten, some 150 years ago, and this is still the very best cocoa available. Although it is more expensive than some other brands, it is definitely worth using for ice cream and chocolate sauces.

BELOW: *cocoa powder*

Milk chocolate

Mild and creamy, milk chocolate is made with up to 40 per cent milk or milk products and contains less cocoa solids than dark chocolate. Because it has a mild flavour, you will need to add more than when using dark chocolate, to obtain a strong flavour. You can use a combination of melted milk chocolate and chopped milk chocolate. As with white chocolate, the addition of milk products means that it requires more careful heating than dark chocolate.

Carob

Although not a true chocolate, carob is viewed by many as an acceptable alternative. It is the ground seedpod of the carob or locust tree and can be used as a chocolate substitute. It is available from health-food stores in bars or in powdered form as a flour. Unlike chocolate, it does not contain any caffeine. If you are using a bar, be cautious as it is highly concentrated. The flour can be used in a similar way to cocoa, but unlike cocoa, it is narurally sweet.

STORING CHOCOLATE

Wrap opened packs of chocolate well or pack them in a plastic box. Store in a cool, dry place away from foods with very strong flavours, such as spices, which may taint the chocolate. Avoid very cold places, or the chocolate may develop a dull whitish bloom. Chocolate has a long shelf life, but check use-by dates before cooking.

Fruits

Berry fruits

TYPES/FORMS: Berry fruits make marvellous ice creams and sorbets. You can choose from standard raspberries, larger tayberries and loganberries, bright red strawberries and tiny alpine and Hautbois strawberries, blueberries, flavoursome blackberries, black, red and white currants, tart green gooseberries and the more unusual red gooseberries. Look out for golden raspberries, too. These tend to be grown in small quantities by keen gardeners and are often difficult to find in the shops, but they are well worth trying when available. As their short midsummer season is soon over, enjoy them while they are available fresh and bursting with rich flavour.

USES: Delicious in ice creams, sorbets and sherbets, berry fruits can also easily be transformed into superb sauces and coulis. Melba sauce is an obvious example, but there are plenty more to choose from. A delectable iced summer pudding that teams sliced fresh strawberries with strawberry ice cream and soft fruit sorbet makes perfect use of summer fruits. Blueberries, red berries and currants look most attractive sprinkled over ice cream sundaes or crushed and added to just setting ice cream for added texture and colour. Expensive alpine and Hautbois strawberries can be used for decoration only.

RIGHT: *redcurrants*

MAKING A PURÉE

Purée berry fruits in a food processor or blender until smooth, then press the purée through a sieve (strainer) into a large bowl, using the back of a large spoon or ladle.

PREPARATION: Press ripe raspberries, tayberries, loganberries, strawberries and blueberries through a fine sieve (strainer) to remove the seeds, then use the purée in ice creams, sherbets or sorbets. These fruit purées are also delicious simply spooned over vanilla ice cream or mixed with a sugar syrup and lemon juice for a refreshing ice cream sauce.

The simplest way to remove currants from their stems is to run the tines (prongs) of a fork gently down the stem over a bowl. As blackcurrants have such a sharp flavour, it is wise to poach them first with sugar or honey and a little water until just tender. Red and white currants can be used as decoration and eaten raw, or lightly poached to make a sauce.

Gooseberries should be topped and tailed with scissors before being cooked with a little sugar or honey. Purée and sieve (strain) currants or cooked gooseberries if adding to ice cream, sorbet or sherbet. Gooseberry ice cream made with clotted cream is a wonderful summertime treat that should not be missed.

Orchard fruits

TYPES/FORMS: Choose from apples, pears, plums, damsons, cherries, apricots, peaches and nectarines.

USES: Orchard fruits, particularly peaches and nectarines, make irresistible ices. Use them in creamy ice creams, sorbets and similar desserts, with a little liqueur, if you like.

PREPARATION: Apples and pears should be peeled and cored; plums, peaches and apricots should be halved and stoned (pitted). The fruit should then be poached in a little water and sugar until tender before being processed to a smooth purée. Ripe peaches, nectarines and apricots can be puréed raw, then sieved (strained) to remove the skins. Damsons are small and difficult to prepare, so poach, then scoop out the stones (pits). Alternatively, press the cooked fruit through a sieve (strainer) to remove the stones. Use stoned cherries whole or roughly chopped. Larger fruits can be used for decoration, provided they are ripe. Slice or chop them, and toss apples and pears in a little lemon juice to prevent discoloration.

How to stone and string cherries

1 Remove cherry stones easily with this handy gadget, which pushes the stones out of the fruit. Usually available from good cookshops.

Citrus fruits

TYPES/FORMS: Choose from lemons, limes, oranges, tangerines, clementines, kumquats and grapefruit.

USES: All citrus fruits can be used to make sorbets, granitas and sherbets. In addition to these uses, oranges make a very good ice cream. Citrus fruit can also be used to make tangy sauces, and the rind is frequently used as a decoration, either as it is or when it has been crystallized.

PREPARATION: Grate the rind or pare it thinly, taking care to remove only the coloured skin, leaving the bitter white pith behind. Cut the fruit in half and squeeze it, then pour the juice through a sieve (strainer) to remove any pips (seeds). Mix it with cream and custard for ice cream or with sugar syrup for sorbets, sherbets and granitas. Kumquats can be poached whole or in slices and used to make a refreshing accompaniment to iced desserts.

2 Cherries threaded on a skewer or cocktail stick (toothpick) make an attractive decoration, especially for an iced drink.

RIGHT: *halved lemons and limes*

Rhubarb

TYPES/FORMS: Strictly speaking, these pretty pink stems are not a fruit at all, but they are used like a fruit in desserts. For making iced desserts, choose the young, slender, baby-pink stems of early forced rhubarb, as it has a much more delicate flavour. Maincrop rhubarb has thicker, darker stems and a coarser texture.

USES: Puréed cooked rhubarb can be used to make an excellent sorbet and granita, or flavour it with ginger for an old-fashioned ice cream. Lightly poached rhubarb can be served as an accompaniment to vanilla, cinnamon or goat's milk ice cream.

PREPARATION: Both early forced and maincrop rhubarb should be cooked with sugar and just a tablespoon or two of water. Put the rhubarb, sugar and water in a heavy-bottomed pan and cook gently for about 30 minutes, or until the rhubarb has softened.

Melons

TYPES/FORMS: Choose from cantaloupe, Charentais, Galia and Ogen melons. Test them for ripeness by pressing the stalk area of the skin. The melon should yield under your thumb and smell quite perfumed.

USES: With their delicate perfume, melons make the most wonderfully refreshing sorbets and granitas. The shells make excellent and attractive containers for serving melon ices.

PREPARATION: Cut the melon in half, scoop out the seeds, then purée the flesh before use. Watermelons can also be used, but as the seeds are speckled throughout the flesh it is often easier to leave them in when processing the fruit. Sieving (straining) the purée after it has been processed will remove them. As watermelons have rather a bland flavour, mix the purée with grated lime rind and juice.

How to segment an orange or a grapefruit

1 Using a sharp knife, start by cutting a slice off the top and bottom of the orange or grapefruit so that you just can see the flesh inside.

2 Using a small serrated knife, slice off the skin and pith cleanly. Work your way from the top down to the base of the fruit.

3 Holding the fruit over a bowl to catch the juices, carefully cut between the membranes to remove the whole fruit segments.

Tropical fruits

TYPES/FORMS: Choose from bananas, pineapples, mangoes, passion fruit, grapes and kiwi fruit. These fruits are now available year-round and are a welcome alternative to seasonal fruits.

USES: Mash or purée peeled bananas with a little grated or pared lemon or lime rind – to prevent discoloration – and make them into smooth ice creams by combining with honey, ginger, chocolate or cinnamon. Puréed or chopped pineapple flesh makes wonderful ice cream, especially when chunky pieces of crushed meringue or a few tablespoons of rum are added. Pineapple can also be puréed and made into tangy sorbets. Look out for the extra sweet varieties, with their bright yellow, juicy flesh. Mix puréed mango with ginger, lime or coconut for a sorbet with a Caribbean flavour. Grapes and kiwi fruit are best served as a colourful accompaniment to iced desserts, although both can be made into sorbet.

PREPARATION: Sliced or diced tropical fruits can be used as a decoration or sautéed in a little butter and sugar and then flamed in a little brandy, rum or orange liqueur for an easy ice cream accompaniment. To prepare pineapples, slice the top off the pineapple, then cut it into slices of the desired width. Cut away the rind with a small sharp knife. Cut away any remaining eyes from the edges of the pineapple slices. Remove the central core of each slice with an apple corer, pastry cutter or knife.

PREPARING PASSION FRUITS

Passion fruits are easy to prepare. Just slice them in half and scoop out the fragrant seeds with a teaspoon. If necessary, press the pulp through a sieve (strainer).

Preparing a mango

1 Place the mango, narrow side down, on a board. Cut a thick, lengthways slice off the sides, keeping the knife blade as close to the central stone as possible. Turn the mango around and repeat on the other side.

2 Make criss-cross cuts in the mango flesh, cutting down only as far as the skin, then turn the large slices of mango inside out so that the diced flesh stands proud. Scoop it into a bowl.

3 Cut all the remaining fruit away from the stone (pit), remove the skin and dice the flesh.

Dried fruits

TYPES/FORMS: Sultanas (golden raisins), raisins, prunes, apricots, peaches, dates and figs are all suitable for use in ice creams, as are dried apples and pears, although these are seldom used for making ice creams and sorbets. Several types of dried fruit – such as apricots, figs and dates – are sold in vacuum packs labelled "ready to eat" and these do not need soaking before use, although they are sometimes macerated in wine or liqueur for extra flavour. More unusual dried fruit includes mango, cranberries and blueberries, all of which can provide an unusual twist to simple family favourites.

USES: Using dried fruits in ice creams is nothing new – rum and raisin is a classic combination. Drying seasonal fruits such as peaches and apricots intensifies their flavour, so they make excellent purées once they have been soaked in fruit juice or alcohol. These can then either be incorporated in ice creams or sorbets, or used as sauces for any ice cream dessert.

PREPARATION: Use the smaller varieties of dried fruit whole or chopped, and steep them in fruit juice, wine, spirits or liqueur if you like. For the best results, ensure that the fruit is totally submerged in the liquid and leave to soak overnight. The smaller varieties do not need to then be puréed before being used. Larger fruits such as apricots and peaches must be soaked overnight and then puréed before being added to ice cream or used as a topping, although chopped fruit can be added when the ice cream is partially frozen to give extra texture and colour.

Glacé fruits and candied peel

These vibrant, jewel-like fruits make a pretty addition to partially frozen ice cream, and are the traditional flavouring in classic Italian Tutti Frutti Ice Cream. They can also be used to decorate elaborate ice cream sundaes. Most fruits can be glacéd (candied), and a wide selection is available in supermarkets and cookshops. Choose from glacé cherries of various colours, glacé or candied pineapple and candied fruit peels. Large whole or sliced glacé fruits tend to be expensive, but are great for special occasion desserts. Sugar is a natural preservative, and glacé fruits will keep well in an airtight container, but they are best used as soon as possible and purchased fresh as needed.

Using glacé fruits

Use a small, sharp knife to finely chop the glacé (candied) fruits, then fold into just setting vanilla ice cream for a classic Tutti Frutti.

Nuts

TYPES/FORMS: Choose from a wide range of whole shelled nuts such as almonds, hazelnuts, pistachios, walnuts and pecans, plus the less widely used macadamias, Brazil nuts, chestnuts and unsalted peanuts.

USES: Nuts are most popular in cream-based ice creams and are seldom added to water ices. Add chunky toasted nuts or nut brittle (praline) for extra crunch in ice creams, or sprinkle them over elaborate ice cream sundaes. Roughly chopped sugared almonds with pastel-coloured coatings look good and make an easy decoration when scattered on top of scoops of home-made ice cream. Ground nuts infused in milk or cream give a delicate flavour to ice creams that are inspired by recipes from the Middle East.

PREPARATION: Toast the nuts, chop them roughly and fold them into partially frozen ice cream. Alternatively, use them to make nut brittle, which can be broken up and folded into ice cream that is on the verge of setting. Finely ground almonds or cashews can be added to just boiled milk or cream, then left to cool. The flavoured milk can then be strained or used as it is to make a custard-based ice cream.

BELOW: *Pistachio nuts are an attractive addition to ice cream.*

Blanching nuts

1 Put nuts such as pistachios, hazelnuts or almonds into a bowl and pour over just enough boiling water to cover. Leave them to stand for a minute or two until the skins expand and soften.

COOK'S TIP *Canned coconut milk combines full flavour and convenience for an ice cream that tastes good and is very easy to make. Reduced-fat varieties provide a healthy alternative, and coconut milk powder can also be used.*

2 Drain the nuts. To pop nuts such as almonds out of their skins, simply pinch them. Skin hazelnuts or pistachios by tipping them into a clean, dry dish towel and rubbing them together vigorously.

Toasting nuts

For maximum flavour, toast whole or roughly chopped nuts in a dry frying pan on the hob (stovetop), in a shallow cake pan (tin) under a hot grill (broiler) or on a baking sheet in a medium oven for just a few minutes, until golden and lightly roasted. You don't need to add oil as the nuts have such a high natural oil content. You can then grind or chop the nuts. Desiccated (dry unsweetened shredded) coconut can also be toasted in this way, but because it is so finely processed you will need to keep a very close eye on it. It browns in a matter of seconds.

Spread out whole, thinly sliced or roughly chopped nuts on a baking tin or sheet. Grill (broil) for 3–4 minutes, shaking the tin or sheet frequently so that the nuts brown evenly all over and don't burn. Leave to cool before either mixing into partially frozen ice cream or scattering on top once the ice cream has been scooped into dishes or cones.

Making nut brittle (praline)

1 Put granulated sugar, whole nuts and a little water into a heavy frying pan. Heat gently, without stirring. Do not use caster (superfine) sugar and do not stir as this would cause the sugar to crystallize, making it solidify and become opaque. Continue to heat the sugar, but don't be tempted to stir the mixture with a spoon. Tilt the pan gently if necessary, to mix any sugar that has not dissolved completely.

2 Keep a watchful eye over the nuts as the sugar and nuts begin to turn golden. Remember to keep the heat low.

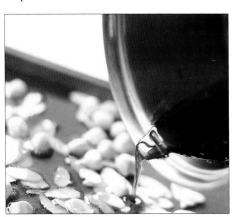

3 Quickly pour a thin layer of the hot nut brittle (praline) mixture on to a cool, oiled baking sheet. Leave to cool and harden before removing as a single large layer.

4 Cover the cooled nut brittle with clear film (plastic wrap) or put it in a strong plastic bag. Break it into rough pieces with a wooden rolling pin.

5 If finely ground nut brittle is needed, you can either crush it further using a rolling pin or grind it up finely in a food processor or coffee grinder.

Other flavourings

Coffee

Iced desserts can be made successfully with freshly-made filter coffee or good instant coffee. Strong filter or espresso coffee is preferable for coffee granita, while coffee ice cream can be made with cracked coffee beans. Bring milk or cream to the boil, add the beans and infuse them, then strain the mixture and use the flavoured milk as the basis for the custard in the ice cream. Another way to make coffee ice cream is by blending cold, strong filter coffee or instant coffee dissolved in a very small amount of water with thick custard and cream. While cracked coffee beans give perhaps the best flavour and a pretty speckled finish (after straining), it can be difficult to judge quantities, so this method is more demanding. If too many beans are used or the custard is overcooked, the finished ice cream can be bitter.

Spirits and liqueurs

The addition of a favourite spirit such as brandy, Calvados or whisky to ice cream, gin or vodka to sorbet, or an orange-flavoured liqueur to a fruity granita can lift a simple iced dessert into the realms of gourmet dining. While it is important to add sufficient alcohol to flavour the mixture (bearing in mind that freezing will dull the flavour), it is also vital to note that too much alcohol can prevent the ice cream or sorbet from freezing hard.

Purists or professional ice cream makers test the density and balance of an ice cream before freezing, using a saccharometer, but a beer-making hydrometer may also be used. This enables the level of sugar to liquid to be checked, ensuring satisfactory freezing. The home cook is unlikely to go to these lengths, and the best guide when adapting or making up recipes is to

taste the mixture before freezing. If it is bland, don't add extra spirit, but pour a little over the ice cream just before serving.

> **FLAVOURING DURING FREEZING**
>
> To add additional flavour, colour and texture, nut brittle (praline), sugared breadcrumbs, crumbled cookies or brownies, diced chocolate, diced glacé fruits or brandy-soaked dried fruits can be folded into semi-frozen ice cream. Transfer the ice cream from the ice cream machine to a plastic tub or a similar freezerproof container when it is thick, but still soft, before folding in the chosen flavouring. (Some machines are capable of mixing in chunky ingredients without being damaged.)

ABOVE: *Spirits and liqueurs can be used in small quantities to add flavour to ice creams.*

Honey

To make enough honey to fill a single standard-size pot, bees have to visit more than two million flowers. The type of flowers and the time of harvest determine the flavour, colour and texture of the finished honey. You can choose from clover, lavender or heather honey, and cheaper blends are also available that include honey from more than one country. Clear heather honey has the best flavour for making ice cream and tastes especially delicious mixed with goat's milk.

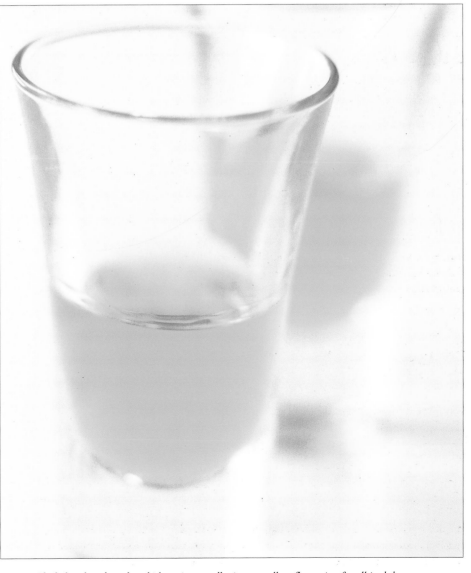

ABOVE: *Alcohol such as brandy, whiskey, gin or vodka is an excellent flavouring for all iced desserts.*

Basic techniques

Making ice creams and sorbets is incredibly easy and satisfying if you use an ice cream maker. The basic techniques are outlined here, but in the first instance, it is vital that you read the handbook supplied with your own machine to ensure that you achieve the best possible results.

FREEZER ASSISTED ICE CREAM MAKERS

Before using the machine, ensure that the bowl or bucket is completely clean and sterile, otherwise bacteria could be transferred to the ice cream. If you are unsure about how clean it is, then wash the inside with hot soapy water using a sponge, rinse with cold water and then wipe dry using kitchen paper. The bowl or bucket must then be placed in the freezer for the time stipulated in your handbook (usually up to 24 hours).

Manufacturers often recommend that you store the bowl or bucket in the freezer so that is ready for immediate use at all times and so that it doesn't take up too much cupboard space. With some machines it is recommended that you wrap the container in a plastic bag first.

1 Make the ice cream, frozen yogurt or sorbet mixture, ensuring that the quantity is suitable for the capacity of your machine. Pour it into a jug (pitcher) and cool it in the refrigerator or freezer until the machine has been set up.

2 Remove the bowl or bucket from the freezer and shake it gently to ensure that the refrigerant is frozen solid. If it is designed to fit inside a casing, lower it into position. Fit the dasher and motor and switch it on.

3 With the dasher rotating, pour the chilled ice cream mixture through the aperture in the lid of the machine in a steady stream, using a rubber or plastic spatula to make sure that all of the mixture is added.

4 During freezing, check the mixture often. Depending on the ingredients used, the temperature at which they were added and the ambient air temperature, the ice cream will be ready in 25–40 minutes. Sorbet freezes more quickly than a rich custard ice cream. Add extra ingredients, like chopped ginger, chocolate or crushed cookies, just before the ice cream is ready.

5 As soon as the mixture is thick and creamy, ladle out the ice cream into dishes or an airtight plastic container. You should try to use a plastic spoon so as not to scratch the container. The ice cream can be served immediately, but it will be quite soft. It will firm up a little more if you leave it in the ice cream maker or put it in the freezer for up to 10 minutes.

6 For ice cream that is firm enough for scooping, scrape the mixture into a tub and chill in the freezer for 2–3 hours. It will keep in the freezer for up to two months, but for the best flavour you should aim to use it within two weeks. Ensure that you label the tub with the type of ice cream and the date on which it was made.

FREE STANDING ICE CREAM MACHINES

With this type of machine, which has its own built-in compressor, there is no need for lengthy pre-freezing, but before you use it for the first time, it is important to leave the machine to stand on a level surface for 24 hours, to allow the refrigerant to settle. If you wanted to, you could prepare the ice cream mixture and chill it in the refrigerator so that it is ready for immediate use after the 24 hour period.

Most free-standing machines have additional removable buckets for making smaller amounts of mixture (up to 600ml|1 pint|2½ cups). For making larger quantities of ice cream (not more than 900ml|1½ pints|3¾ cups), use the fixed bowl.

TIP *One word of warning – when you first start to use a machine of this type, it is all too easy to turn off the compressor instead of turning on the dasher motor. If you do this inadvertently – or if there is a power cut – it is vital to wait at least 10 minutes before starting it again. This is because the compressor has a safety device to prevent any damage to the motor unit. If you switch the machine on immediately, the compressor will appear to be working but it will not freeze.*

1 Switch on the freezer unit (compressor) at least 10 minutes before adding the ice cream mixture. If you are using the removable bucket, pour the recommended quantity of alcohol into the fixed bowl. This will act as a conductor, speeding up the freezing process.

2 If you are using the bucket rather than the bowl, fit it in place inside the machine casing. Insert the appropriate dasher (there will probably be separate dashers of different sizes for the bucket or bowl).

4 With the dasher rotating, pour the chilled mixture in a steady trickle through the aperture in the lid so that it flows into the bucket or bowl. Once you have poured all of the mixture in, the ice cream, frozen yogurt or sorbet will be ready in 20–40 minutes. When the iced mixture has reached the correct consistency, switch off the dasher motor and lift off the lid and dasher.

3 Close the lid, lowering it gently over the lid and motor unit so that it connects with the dasher spindle. Switch on the dasher motor, being careful not to accidentally turn off the compressor motor.

5 For slightly firmer ice cream, the motor operating the compressor or freezing unit can be left on for 5–10 minutes more, but do not leave it on for longer than this or the ice cream will become too solid to remove from the container. Scoop out the ice cream with a plastic spoon. Serve at once or transfer to a tub and place in the freezer.

TIPS FOR USING AN ICE CREAM MAKER

- Try to always use good-quality ingredients whenever possible.
- Always pre-chill the machine or the double-skinned bowl for the time recommended. If possible, keep the bowl or machine in the freezer all of the time.
- To get the best results make sure that you chill the mixture thoroughly before churning in the ice cream maker.
- Use only the quantities stipulated in your handbook. Air will be incorporated during churning so there must be plenty of room for expansion.
- Add extra ingredients only when the ice cream is already starting to thicken. Check that your machine can cope before adding large chunks.
- Clean your ice cream machine very carefully before putting it away, and wash before using if it has been in storage for a while. Good kitchen practice is particularly important when dealing with dairy products.

STORING

- For maximum flavour, don't store your ice cream at all. Eat it right away. If it is too soft for your liking, leave it in the ice cream machine for 10 minutes or so to firm up.
- If you do want or need to store your ice cream, use a clean freezerproof container with a tight-fitting lid, and which is the correct size for the volume of ice cream you wish to store. When filling, leave a little headspace at the top of the mixture to allow for expansion during freezing. Label the container with the type of ice cream and the date on which it was made.
- If the container is only part-filled, either because you do not have a container of a suitable size, or because you've already removed some of the ice cream, cover the surface of the ice cream with clear film (plastic wrap) to prevent the formation of ice crystals.
- Home-made ice cream contains no preservatives or stabilizers, so will not keep for as long as the commercial product. For the best flavour, it is preferable to use home-made ice cream within two weeks. Do not store for longer than two months.

Basic recipes

Many classic ice creams are based on a custard made from eggs and milk. It is not difficult to make, but as it is used so frequently, it is worth perfecting by following these very simple guidelines.

Classic custard base

Making the custard base for ice cream

INGREDIENTS

FLAVOURING to INFUSE (optional)

300ml|½ pint|1¼ cups
SEMI-SKIMMED (LOW-FAT) MILK

4 EGG YOLKS

75g|3oz|6 tbsp CASTER (SUPERFINE) SUGAR

5ml|1 tsp CORNFLOUR (CORNSTARCH)

BATCH COOKING

If you are planning to make ice cream for a party, make double quantities of custard to save time. It is not advisable, however, to increase the quantities any more than this, or it would be difficult to heat the custard evenly. It is quicker and easier to make up two double-quantity batches in separate pans and a lot safer than running the risk of curdling one pan of custard made with a dozen eggs!

---

1 Prepare any flavourings. Split vanilla pods (beans) with a sharp knife; crack coffee beans with a mallet. Cinnamon sticks, whole cloves, fresh rosemary and lavender sprigs or bay leaves can be used as they are.

2 Pour the milk into a pan. Bring it to the boil, then remove the pan from the heat, add the chosen flavouring and leave to infuse for 30 minutes or until cool.

3 If you have used a vanilla pod, lift it out of the pan, and scrape the seeds back into the milk to enrich the flavour. Whisk the egg yolks, caster sugar and cornflour in a bowl until thick and foamy. Bring the plain or infused milk to the boil, then gradually whisk it into the yolk mixture. Carefully pour the combined mixture back into the pan.

4 Cook the mixture over a low heat, stirring it continuously until it approaches boiling point and thickens to the point where the custard will coat the back of a wooden spoon. Do not let the custard overheat or it may curdle. Take the pan off the heat and continue stirring, making sure to take the spoon right around the bottom edges of the pan.

5 Pour the custard into a bowl and cover the surface with clear film (plastic wrap) with a light sprinkling of caster sugar to prevent the formation of a skin. Leave to cool, then chill until required. When making the ice cream in a machine, chill the custard for 1–2 hours in the refrigerator or 20 minutes in the freezer.

6 Follow the preliminary instructions for your specific ice cream maker, pre-cooling the machine or chilling the bowl in the freezer. Stir whipping cream, whipped double (heavy) cream or any soft cream cheeses into the chilled plain or flavoured custard, and then churn until firm.

COOK'S TIP *Reduce the temperature of custard by pouring it into a cool bowl. Stand this in a larger bowl of cold or iced water and change the water as it warms.*

Parfait

Making a basic parfait

Made correctly, a parfait is a light, cream-based confection with a softer, smoother texture than ice cream. Unlike ice cream, it does not need beating during freezing.

Parfaits are traditionally set in moulds, tall glasses, china dishes or, more recently, in edible chocolate cups. The secret of a good parfait lies in the sugar syrup. Dissolve the sugar gently without stirring so that it does not crystallize, then boil it rapidly until it registers 115°C| 239°F on a sugar thermometer, or when a small amount of the syrup, dropped into a cup of cold water, solidifies and can be moulded into a ball.

Quickly whisk the syrup into the whisked eggs. Cook over hot water until very thick. Cool, then mix with flavourings, alcohol and whipped cream. Freeze until solid and serve straight from the freezer.

SERVES FOUR

INGREDIENTS

115g|4oz|generous ½ cup CASTER (SUPERFINE) SUGAR

120ml|4fl oz|½ cup WATER

4 EGG YOLKS

FLAVOURINGS

300ml|½ pint|1¼ cups DOUBLE (HEAVY) CREAM

1 Mix the sugar and water in a pan. Heat the pan gently, without stirring, until the sugar has dissolved completely. Meanwhile, half fill a medium pan with water and bring it to simmering point.

2 Bring the sugar syrup to the boil and boil it rapidly for 4–5 minutes until it starts to thicken. It will be ready to use when it registers 115°C|239°F on a sugar thermometer, or will form a soft ball when dropped into water.

FLAVOURINGS

Traditionally flavoured with coffee or chocolate and a dash of brandy or whisky, parfaits are also delicious made with ground spices such as cinnamon with apple or ginger with banana. Double (heavy) cream adds just the right degree of richness and a velvety texture, although crème fraîche or whipping cream can also be used with very good results. Another traditional combination is a fruit purée mixed with a liqueur such as kirsch, Cointreau or Grand Marnier; these make a sophisticated iced dessert at a dinner party.

---

3 Put the egg yolks in a heatproof bowl and whisk until light and frothy. Place the bowl over the simmering water and gradually whisk in the hot sugar syrup. Whisk steadily until creamy. Take off the heat and continue whisking until cool, when the whisk leaves a trail across the surface when lifted.

4 Fold in the chosen flavourings, such as melted chocolate and brandy, ground cinnamon and coffee, whisky and chopped ginger, kirsch and raspberry purée or kir and strawberry purée. In a separate bowl, whip the cream lightly until it just holds its shape. Fold it into the mixture with a metal spoon, being careful not to knock out too much air.

5 Pour the parfait mixture into prepared moulds, dishes or chocolate-lined cases. Place in the freezer and leave for at least 4 hours or overnight, until firm. Decorate, if liked, with whipped cream, spoonfuls of crème fraîche, caramel shapes or chocolate-dipped fruits. Serve immediately.

COOK'S TIP *Double (heavy) cream adds just the right degree of richness to parfaits, although crème fraîche or whipping cream can also be used as a lighter or lower-fat alternative.*

Making water ices

Sorbets are made with a light sugar syrup flavoured with fruit juice, fruit purée, wine, liqueur, tea or herbs. They should not contain milk or cream (ingredients found in sherbets), and are best made in an ice cream maker, as the constant churning ensures that the ice crystals are as tiny as possible.

Sorbet

Making a basic sorbet

SERVES SIX

INGREDIENTS

150–200g|5–7oz|¾–1cup CASTER (SUPERFINE) SUGAR

200–300ml|7–10fl oz|¾–1¼ cups WATER

FLAVOURING

1 EGG WHITE

FRUIT PURÉES

As an approximate guide, 500g|1¼lb|5 cups of berry fruits will produce about 450ml|¾ pint|scant 2 cups purée. Mix this with 115g–150g|4–5oz|generous ½–¾ cup caster (superfine) sugar (depending on the natural acidity of the fruit), which has been dissolved in 300ml|½ pint|1¼ cups boiling water and then made up to 1 litre|1¾ pints|4 cups with extra cold water, lemon or lime juice.

---

1 Put the sugar and water in a medium pan and heat the mixture, stirring, until the sugar has just dissolved.

2 Add pared citrus rinds, herbs or spices, depending on your chosen flavouring. Leave to infuse. Strain and cool, then chill well in the refrigerator. Add extra flavourings such as fruit juices, sieved puréed fruits, herbs or tea.

3 Having prepared your ice cream maker, pour the syrup mixture into the machine with the dasher rotating and churn until it is thick but still too soft to scoop.

4 Lightly beat the egg white with a fork and pour it into the ice cream maker, either adding it through the top vent or removing the lid and stirring it in, depending on the method recommended by the manufacturer of your machine. Continue churning the sorbet until it is firm enough to scoop with a spoon.

5 BY HAND: Pour the mixture into a plastic tub or similar freezerproof container. It should not be more than 4cm|1½in deep. Cover and freeze in the coldest part of the freezer for 4 hours or until it has partially frozen and ice crystals have begun to form. Beat until smooth with a fork, or hand-held electric whisk. Alternatively, process in a food processor until smooth.

6 BY HAND: Lightly beat the egg white and stir it into the sorbet. Freeze for a further 4 hours or until firm enough to scoop.

COOK'S TIP *If making by hand, ensure that the freezer temperature is as low as possible to speed up the freezing process, and beat at regular intervals.*

Granita

Making a citrus granita

This wonderfully refreshing, simple Italian-style water ice has the fine texture of snow and is most often served piled into pretty glass dishes. You don't need your ice cream machine, just a medium pan, a sieve (strainer) or blender for puréeing the fruit, a fork and room in the freezer for a large plastic container.

INGREDIENTS

There are no hard-and-fast rules when it comes to the proportions of sugar to water, nor is there a standard amount of flavouring which must be added. Unlike sorbets, granitas consist largely of water, with just enough sugar to sweeten them and prevent them from freezing too hard. A total of 1 litre|1¾ pints|4 cups of flavoured sugar syrup will provide six generous portions of granita.

1 Squeeze the juice from six lemons, oranges or four ruby grapefruits. Add 115–200g|4–7oz| generous ½–1 cup caster (superfine) sugar, depending on the natural acidity of the fruit. Dissolve the sugar in 300ml|½ pint|1¼ cups boiling water, then mix it with the citrus juice and rind. Top up to 1 litre|1¾ pints|4 cups with extra water or water and alcohol. Add enough alcohol to taste but don't be over generous or the granita will not freeze.

2 Pour the chilled mixture into a large plastic tub or similar freezerproof container. It should not be more than 2–2.5cm|¾–1in deep. Freeze it in the coldest part of the freezer for 2 hours until it is mushy around the edges.

Take the container out of the freezer and beat the granita well with a fork to break up the ice crystals. Return the granita to the freezer. Beat it at 30 minute intervals for the next 2 hours until it has the texture of snow.

Making a hot infusion

Some of the most delicious granitas are based on hot mixtures. Coffee is just one example. Pour hot, strong filtered coffee into a bowl or pan and stir in sugar to taste. For a ginger granita, infuse finely chopped root ginger in boiling water, then sweeten it. Chocolate granita is made by mixing unsweetened cocoa powder to a smooth paste with a little boiling water and sweetening to taste. All hot infusions must be left to cool, then chilled before being frozen.

Making a fruit-flavoured granita

To make a fruit-flavoured granita, purée berry fruits such as raspberries or strawberries, then sieve (strain) the purée to remove the seeds. Alternatively, purée ripe peaches, then sieve to remove the skins. To make a melon granita, scoop the seeds out of orange- or green-fleshed melons, then purée the flesh. Peeled and seeded watermelon can be puréed in the same way, or the flesh can be puréed along with the seeds and then sieved afterwards.

> **SERVING AND STORING GRANITAS**
>
> Coffee granita is classically served in a tumbler with a spoonful of whipped cream on top. Other types of granita look pretty spooned into tall glasses and decorated with fresh fruits or herb leaves and flowers. Because of its soft, snow-like texture, a granita is best served as soon as it is made. If this is not possible, you can leave it for a couple of hours in the freezer, beating it once or twice more if convenient. If you must freeze a granita overnight or for even longer, let it thaw slightly and beat it really well with a fork before serving. The ice crystals will become smaller but the taste will be the same. As a granita does not contain dairy products there are fewer concerns about food contamination or deterioration.

COOK'S TIP *Before you make the granita, make sure that the container you choose will fit in your freezer. A new stainless-steel roasting pan can be used to freeze the granita mixture. As this metal is such a good conductor, the granita will freeze very much faster than it would in a plastic container. Do not use aluminium, as the metal could react with the fruit acids to give a metallic taste to the finished granita.*

Layering and rippling

For a professional look and a dramatic effect, create different layers of harmonizing ice creams in large or small, rectangular or round moulds. There are plenty of possibilities – just let your imagination take over.

How to layer ices

Simple three-tier ice cream

1 When the first flavour has thickened and is semi-frozen, pour it into a 25 x 7.5 x 7.5cm| 10 x 3 x 3in terrine or loaf tin (pan) that has been lined with clear film (plastic wrap). Spread it in an even layer and freeze it in the coldest part of the freezer for 1 hour or until firm.

2 Pour in the second layer of semi-frozen ice cream and spread it out evenly. Freeze until firm, then add the final ice cream layer and freeze for 4–5 hours until hard. When ready to serve, turn out the ice cream from the mould, peel off the clear film and cut the terrine into slices, using a warm knife.

Chequerboard

1 Make a two-tier terrine, using two of your favourite ice creams layered in a terrine or straight-sided 900g|2lb loaf pan. Invert the two-tier terrine on a board and cut it in half lengthways, using a hot knife.

2 Turn one of the halves over to reverse the colour sequence and wrap tightly in clear film to stick them together. Refreeze to harden. To serve, peel away the clear film and slice with a hot knife.

Iced roulade

1 Prepare two quantities of semi-frozen ice cream with flavours that complement each other well. Line a 30 x 23cm|12 x 9in baking sheet with clear film (plastic wrap) or waxed paper. Spread one quantity of thick, semi-frozen, flavoured ice cream. Freeze for 20 minutes.

2 Spoon the second batch of semi-frozen ice cream over a second piece of clear film or waxed paper to make a rectangle a little smaller than the first. Freeze for 20 minutes. Carefully place this sheet of ice cream over the first layer, then peel off the clear film or waxed paper.

3 Roll the layered ice cream, as if making a Swiss roll (jelly roll), starting from the longest edge and using the clear film or paper to roll it. Pat the ice cream into a neat cylinder, then wrap it in more clear film. Freeze for several hours, overnight if time permits, until the roll is hard.

4 Peel off the clear film (plastic wrap) or paper and put the roll on a board. Cut it into thick slices, using a warmed knife.

Classic cassata

This classic Italian iced dessert is traditionally made in a rounded metal mould with a lid. If you don't have a metal mould, a plastic or thick glass bowl can be used instead. Do not confuse this ice cream dessert with the Sicilian cake of the same name.

THE HISTORY OF CASSATA

Some people think that cassata is modelled on the dome of the Brunelleschi cathedral in Florence; others believe that the famous dessert was the result of a culinary accident when cream and wine were accidentally spilled into a soldier's metal helmet that was being stored in a chilly cave. Whatever its true origins, cassata is traditionally served in Italy at weddings and Easter celebrations and comprises two or three layers of ice cream, depending on the size of the mould in which it is made.

1 Line a 1.2 litre|2 pint|5 cup bowl with clear film (plastic wrap). Line it with a 2cm|¾in thick layer of semi-frozen strawberry ice cream, using the back of a metal spoon to press the ice cream down firmly against the sides and bottom of the basin. Cover the bowl with clear film and freeze for 1–2 hours or until the ice cream lining is completely firm.

2 Again using the back of a metal spoon, press some chocolate ice cream on to the strawberry ice cream in the mould to make a second 2cm|¾in thick layer of chocolate ice cream against the frozen strawberry layer. Leave a space in the centre. Cover and freeze for a further 1–2 hours or until the chocolate ice cream layer is firm.

3 Pack the centre with tutti frutti ice cream and smooth the top. Cover and freeze overnight until firm. Dip the mould in hot water for 10 seconds, insert a knife between the clear film and the basin, then invert it on to a serving plate. Lift off the basin and peel away the clear film and decorate with glacé (candied) fruits or chocolate caraque. Serve in wedges.

Individual bombes

1 Line four individual metal moulds with clear film, then press a 1cm|½in layer of dark chocolate ice cream over the bottom and sides of each mould, smoothing the ice cream with the back of a teaspoon. Cover and freeze for 30 minutes or until the ice cream is firm.

2 Add a scoop of vanilla ice cream to the centre of each lined mould and insert a brandy-soaked prune or cherry into the middle. Smooth the surface, cover and freeze for 4 hours until firm.

3 Dip the filled moulds into a roasting pan filled with hot water for 2 seconds. Invert the moulds on to serving plates and quickly lift off the metal moulds.

4 Remove the clear film, then decorate the top and sides of each individual bombe with long sweeping lines of piped white chocolate. Serve immediately.

How to ripple ices

This dramatic and eye-catching effect is surprisingly easy to achieve, using ice creams and sauces in contrasting colours, which are lightly swirled together while the ice cream is semi-frozen.

Flavoured ice cream

Choose softly set ice cream that is too soft to scoop but thick enough to hold its shape. The colours should be markedly different for the most dramatic effect.

Sauces

Marble a chocolate, toffee or fruit sauce through ice cream that is on the verge of setting. Be careful with toffee sauces, as they can dissolve into the ice cream, so losing the effect.

Raspberry ripple ice cream

Fruit purée

Puréed and strained fruit purées can be used unsweetened but can taste rather icy. It is better to mix them with a thick sugar syrup before swirling them with semi-frozen ice cream.

Jam

For the easiest rippled ice cream of all, use softly set extra fruit jam straight from the jar. You can use firmer jams, but they will need to be mixed with a little boiling water to soften before being used. Make sure the jam is cold when you use it, or it will melt the ice cream. Any fruit jam can be used but the contrast of berry fruits looks the most attractive.

RIGHT: *Use softly set jam for ice creams.*

1 Make the vanilla ice cream by hand or churn it in an ice cream maker until it is thick but too soft to scoop.

2 Mix 75g|3oz|6 tbsp caster (superfine) sugar with 60ml|4 tbsp water in a pan. Heat until the sugar has dissolved, then boil for 3 minutes until syrupy, but not coloured. Cool slightly. Purée 250g|9oz|1½ cups raspberries in a food processor or blender then press through a sieve (strainer) over a bowl. Stir in the syrup and chill well.

3 Add alternate spoonfuls of the soft, partially frozen vanilla ice cream and the chilled raspberry syrup to a 1 litre|1¾ pint|4 cup plastic tub or similar freezerproof container. Don't be alarmed if the contrasting layers look a little messy to begin with.

4 Stir through the syrup and ice cream two or three times to create a rippled effect. Freeze.

CLASSIC COMBINATIONS

Ripple one of the basic recipes in this book with one of your own favourite flavours. Use the same basic technique as for raspberry ripple.

Mixed berry swirl – strawberry ice cream with raspberry syrup.

Coffee toffee swirl – dark classic coffee ice cream swirled with a rich toffee sauce.

Double chocolate – smooth dark chocolate ice cream rippled with smooth white chocolate ice cream.

Apricot and orange ripple – orange and yogurt ice rippled with apricot sauce.

Creamy toffee ripple – rich toffee sauce rippled through creamy vanilla ice cream.

Raspberry ripple – try the home-made version made with the very best of ingredients for a truly timeless classic.

Marbling ice cream

Although very similar to the technique used when making a rippled ice cream, marbling creates softer, less defined swirls. The same combinations of ice cream and syrup, sauce or purée can be used as for making rippled ice creams, but the softer effect is achieved by mixing together more thoroughly.

1 To achieve this effect, spoon alternate layers of partially frozen ice cream into a plastic tub or similar freezerproof container. Drizzle coloured liquid flavouring or syrup over each layer, using a spoon.

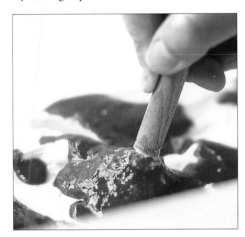

2 Pass the handle of a wooden spoon through the ice cream and liquid flavouring five or six times to produce a lightly marbled effect. Freeze the ice cream for 4–5 hours or overnight, until firm.

COOK'S TIP *Soft marbled ice cream need only be lightly swirled with the end of a spoon to create the required effect. Choose a coloured liquid flavouring that complements the base ice cream in colour and taste.*

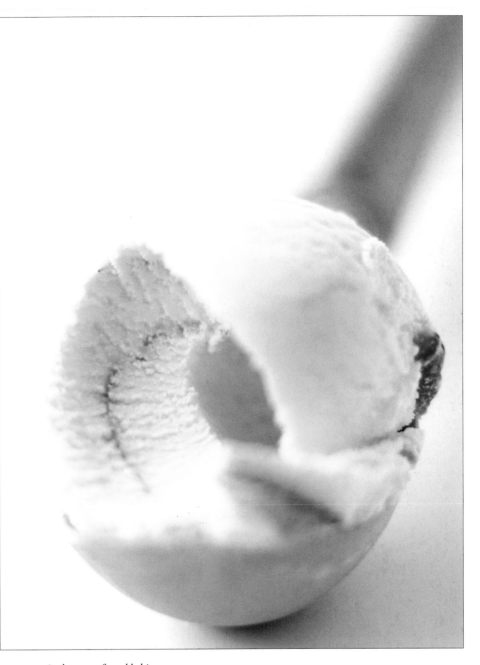

ABOVE: *a single scoop of marbled ice cream*

SECRETS OF SUCCESS

- Line the mould with clear film (plastic wrap) so that it is easy to remove the frozen dessert.

- Choose flavours that contrast or complement each other, such as dark chocolate with pistachio, or vanilla and strawberry.

- Freeze ice cream after each layer has been added so that soft mixtures do not merge together. That way, the finished dessert will have well-defined layers.

- Make sure that the colours of the ice cream are in harmony, but are strong enough to be visible.

- Freeze the mould thoroughly after layering, preferably overnight, so that the layers will not separate when the ice cream is sliced.

- Dip the mould in hot water for 10–15 seconds so that the dessert will turn out easily. Peel off the clear film and use a knife dipped into warm water for slicing.

Baskets and biscuits

Not only beautiful to look at, these sensational edible containers are surprisingly easy to make and are bound to impress your guests. They are the ultimate stylish and professional presentation and taste delicious too.

How to make baskets

Spun sugar baskets

These impressive baskets look stunning filled with ice cream, or upturned and placed over a single scoop of ice cream to form a cage, and arranged in the centre of a large white dinner plate. Use an oiled soup ladle instead of oranges for slightly flatter baskets, and loosen with the tip of a small knife before removing. Add rich colour by decorating the plate with tiny clusters of blueberries, a few raspberries and a sprig or two of redcurrants or any combination of summer fruits. Dust lightly with icing (confectioners') sugar for the final effect.

MAKES SIX

INGREDIENTS

3 ORANGES, to serve as moulds

a little OIL for greasing

250g|9oz|generous 1 cup SUGAR

75ml|5 tbsp WATER

VANILLA ICE CREAM and
FRESH SUMMER FRUITS, to serve

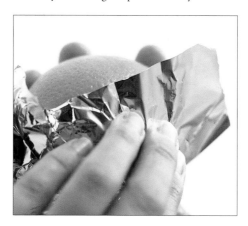

1 Smooth squares of foil over three oranges and brush lightly with oil. Put the granulated sugar and water in a thick-bottomed pan and heat gently, without stirring, until the sugar has completely dissolved. Increase the heat and boil the syrup until it turns golden and starts to caramelize.

2 Take the pan off the heat and plunge the bottom of it into a bowl of cold water to prevent the caramel from continuing to cook and overbrowning. Allow the caramel to cool for 15–30 seconds, stirring it gently until it starts to thicken, then lift the pan out of the water.

3 Hold a foil-wrapped orange over the pan and quickly drizzle caramel from a dessertspoon over half the orange, making squiggly lines and gradually building up layers to make the basket shape. Leave the caramel to set and make a second and third basket in the same way. Warm the caramel when it gets too stiff to drizzle.

4 Ease the foil off the first orange. Carefully peel the foil away and put the finished sugar basket on a lightly oiled baking sheet. Repeat with the remaining baskets, then make three more in the same way, reheating the caramel as needed and adding a little boiling water if it gets too thick to drizzle.

5 Use the baskets on the day you make them, filling them with vanilla ice cream and summer fruits and adding a dusting of sifted icing sugar. The baskets are extremely fragile, so scoop the ice cream on to a plate or baking sheet first and lower it carefully into each basket with the aid of two forks.

Chocolate tulips

These easy-to-make tulip baskets take only minutes to prepare and can then be set aside to harden. Fill with one large scoop of ice cream and decorate with blueberries and halved strawberries, or fill with tiny scoops of ice cream shaped with a melon baller and decorate with tiny chocolate shapes.

VARIATIONS *Any of the chocolate basket ideas suggested here are a perfect way of setting off your favourite chocolate, coffee or vanilla ice cream. You do not have to use dark (bittersweet) chocolate to make the baskets – Belgian white or milk chocolate work just as well.*

1 Using the back of a teaspoon, spread 175g|6oz melted dark (bittersweet) chocolate over six 13cm|5in circles of baking parchment, taking it almost, but not completely, to the edge, and giving it a swirly, wave-like edge.

2 Drape each paper circle, chocolate-side outwards, over an upturned glass tumbler set on a baking sheet. Ease the paper into soft pleats and leave the baskets in a cool place to set. When ready to serve, lift the baskets off the glasses and carefully peel away the paper.

A large chocolate bowl

3 Chill well until set, then carefully peel away the foil and place the bowl on a plate. Store in the refrigerator until ready to fill.

COOK'S TIP *This bowl can be made in any size. Small ones are perfect for individual portions, while larger bowls can serve up to four. Make it thicker than the other bowls and don't fill it too full, or the weight of the ice cream might cause the chocolate to crack.*

1 Smooth a double thickness of foil into a suitably sized mixing bowl or basin, so that it takes on the shape of the container. Carefully lift the foil out of the bowl.

2 Spoon melted chocolate into the bottom of the foil bowl. Spread it to an even, fairly thick layer, taking it over the base and sides with the back of a spoon or a pastry brush.

Individual chocolate cups

3 Fill each of the set chocolate cups with parfait. Chill again in the freezer, then carefully peel away the paper from each cup. Use a palette knife or spatula to transfer each filled cup to a plate, then decorate them with a light dusting of sifted cocoa and serve immediately.

COOK'S TIP *When melting chocolate, it is important that the chocolate isn't overheated or allowed to come into contact with steam or small amounts of moisture, as these will cause it to stiffen or "seize". Make sure that the base of the bowl doesn't touch the water and don't allow the water to boil.*

1 Cut six 30 x 15cm|12 x 6in strips of baking parchment. Fold each strip in half lengthways, roll into a circle and fit it inside a 7.5cm|3in plain biscuit (cookie) cutter to make a collar. Secure with tape. Ease the cutter away and make five more collars, leaving the last collar inside the cutter. Place on a baking sheet.

2 Melt 250g|9oz dark (bittersweet) chocolate in a heatproof bowl over a pan of hot water. Brush chocolate evenly over the base and sides of the paper collar, supported by the biscuit cutter, and make the top edge jagged. Carefully lift off the biscuit cutter and slide over the next paper collar. Make six cups and leave to set.

How to make biscuits

Tuiles

These classic French biscuits (cookies) are named after the similarly shaped roof tiles found on many old French homes.

SERVES SIX

INGREDIENTS

OIL, for greasing

50g|2oz|¼ cup UNSALTED (SWEET) BUTTER

75g|3oz|¾ cup FLAKED (SLICED) ALMONDS

2 EGG WHITES

75g|3oz|6 tbsp CASTER (SUPERFINE) SUGAR

50g|2oz|½ cup PLAIN (ALL-PURPOSE) FLOUR, sifted

RIND of ½ ORANGE, finely grated plus 10ml|2 tsp JUICE

SIFTED ICING (CONFECTIONERS') SUGAR, to decorate

1 Preheat the oven to 200°C|400°F|Gas 6. Lightly brush a wooden rolling pin with oil, and line two large baking sheets with baking parchment. Melt the butter in a pan and set it aside. Preheat the grill (broiler). Spread out the almonds on a baking sheet and lightly brown under the grill. Leave to cool, then finely grind half; crush the remainder roughly with your fingertips.

2 Put the egg whites and sugar in a bowl and lightly fork them together. Sift in the flour, stir gently to mix, then fold in the melted butter, then the orange rind and juice. Fold in the finely ground nuts.

3 Drop six teaspoons of the mixture on to one of the lined baking sheets, spacing them well apart. Spread the mixture into thin circles and sprinkle lightly with the crushed nuts. Bake in the oven for 5 minutes until lightly browned around the edges.

COOK'S TIP *It is important to transfer the tuiles to the rolling pin as quickly as possible. As the biscuits (cookies) cool they will set and become crisp and it will not be possible to shape them.*

4 Loosen one of the biscuits with a slim spatula and drape it over the rolling pin. Shape the remaining biscuits in the same way. Leave for 5 minutes to set while baking a second batch of biscuits. Continue baking and shaping biscuits until all the mixture has been used. Dust with icing sugar and serve with ice cream.

Cigarettes russes

These biscuits (cookies) are smaller and are rolled more tightly than tuiles, but they can be made using the same recipe. Omit the nuts, orange rind and juice. Add 5ml|1 tsp vanilla essence (extract). Make 2–3 biscuits at a time, each time using 10ml|2 tsp of the mixture spread into a thin circle. The mixture makes 15 cigarettes russes. Bake the biscuits until they are golden around the edges, then turn them over and wrap them around lightly oiled wooden spoon handles. Leave for 5 minutes to set.

Brandy snaps

Traditionally rolled into fat cigar shapes, these crisp, lacy biscuits (cookies) can also be made into tiny petits fours or even bowls.

MAKES 32

INGREDIENTS

OIL, for greasing

115g|4oz|½ cup UNSALTED (SWEET) BUTTER

115g|4oz|generous ½ cup CASTER (SUPERFINE) SUGAR

115g|4oz|⅓ cup GOLDEN SYRUP or LIGHT CORN SYRUP

115g|4oz|1 cup PLAIN FLOUR

5ml|1 tsp GROUND GINGER

15ml|1 tbsp LEMON JUICE

15ml|1 tbsp BRANDY

COOK'S TIP *Brandy snaps can be made the day before being served. Store them covered with greaseproof (waxed) paper in a cool, dry place. They can also be frozen. Pack in layers in a rigid plastic box, interleaved with greaseproof paper.*

1 Preheat the oven to 190°C|375°F| Gas 5. Lightly oil the handles of two or three wooden spoons (or more if you have them). Line two large baking sheets with baking parchment. Put the butter, sugar and syrup into a medium pan and heat gently on the hob (stovetop), stirring occasionally until the butter has melted.

2 Once all of the sugar has dissolved and the butter has melted take the pan off the heat and sift in the flour and the ground ginger. Mix together well with a wooden spoon until the mixture is smooth, then stir in the lemon juice and the brandy. Mix well to combine, ensuring that there are no lumps.

4 Quickly roll each brandy snap around the handle of an oiled wooden spoon and put join-side downwards on a wire rack to cool. Leave to set for 1 minute, then remove the spoon from the first biscuit and shape the others on the tray in the same way, by which time the second batch of biscuits will probably be ready.

3 Drop four teaspoons of the mixture on to the lined baking sheets, spacing them well apart. Cook for 5–6 minutes, until they are pale brown, bubbling and the edges are just darkening. Take the tray of biscuits out of the oven, leave them to stand for 15–30 seconds to set slightly, then loosen with a slim spatula.

CHOCOLATE SNAPS

For chocolate brandy snaps substitute 15g|½oz|2 tbsp of sifted cocoa powder for 15g|½oz| 2 tbsp of the flour. Do not use drinking-chocolate powder as this has added sugar and dried milk powder.

Mini brandy snap biscuits for petits fours

1 Spoon half teaspoons of the basic brandy snap mixture on to lined baking sheets and spread thinly to form circles. Bake until golden brown, then shape around oiled wooden satay sticks or metal kebab skewers. Work quickly, as the small biscuits (cookies) will cool rapidly. Leave to set for 5 minutes.

2 For mini cornets, shape the biscuits by wrapping them around oiled cream horn moulds or large piping tubes. Leave for 5 minutes to set. Remove the moulds or piping tubes once the biscuits are cool and dip the ends of the biscuits into melted white or dark chocolate, if liked.

Brandy snap bowls

1 Drop 15ml|1 tbsp of the basic brandy snap mixture on to a lined baking sheet, spread it to a circle and cook for 6–7 minutes. Cool for a few seconds until firm enough to remove. Quickly lift the biscuit and drape it, textured side outwards, over an orange that has been lightly brushed with oil.

2 Flute the edges by easing the biscuit into folds with your fingertips. Leave to cool. As soon as it has set, lift it off the orange.

COOK'S TIP *These bowls are best made one at a time. They cook quickly and are shaped in a couple of minutes.*

Classic ice cream sauces

No ice cream sundae would be complete without one of these popular sauces. For convenience, they can all be made in advance and stored in the refrigerator until needed, and can be served hot or cold, as preferred.

Chocolate sauce

Rich, dark and irresistible. Pour the warm or cold sauce over vanilla or milk chocolate ice cream or serve with an ice cream sundae made with your favourite flavours.

MAKES 400ml | 14fl oz | 1⅔ cups

INGREDIENTS

25g|1oz|2 tbsp BUTTER

25g|1oz|2 tbsp CASTER (SUPERFINE) SUGAR

30ml|2 tbsp GOLDEN SYRUP or
LIGHT CORN SYRUP

200g|7oz LUXURY PLAIN (SEMISWEET)
COOKING CHOCOLATE

150ml|¼ pint|⅔ cup SEMI-SKIMMED
(LOW-FAT) MILK

45ml|3 tbsp DOUBLE (HEAVY) CREAM

1 Mix the butter, sugar and syrup in a pan. Break the plain chocolate into pieces and add it to the mixture. Heat very gently, stirring occasionally, until the chocolate has melted.

2 Gradually stir in the milk and cream and bring just to the boil, stirring constantly until smooth. Serve hot or cool, refrigerate and reheat when required.

Butterscotch sauce

Smooth and glossy, this creamy toffee sauce is extremely rich. It is delicious with vanilla, coffee or yogurt ice creams. Once made, it can be stored in the refrigerator for up to 4 days.

MAKES 475ml | 16fl oz | 2 cups

INGREDIENTS

200g|7oz| 1 cup CASTER (SUPERFINE) SUGAR

45ml|3 tbsp each
COLD WATER and
BOILING WATER

75g|3oz|6 tbsp BUTTER

150ml|¼ pint|⅔ cup DOUBLE (HEAVY) CREAM

1 Put the sugar and 45ml|3 tbsp cold water into a pan and heat very gently, without stirring, until all the sugar has dissolved.

COOK'S TIP *Don't be tempted to stir the sugar syrup when it is boiling or you may find that the sugar will crystallize and solidify. If this happens, the mixture cannot be retrieved. You will have to throw it away and begin again.*

2 Bring the mixture to the boil. Boil until the sugar starts to turn golden, then quickly take the pan off the heat and immediately plunge the bottom of the pan into cold water, to prevent the sugar from overbrowning.

3 Standing as far back as possible, and protecting your hand with an oven glove, add the 45ml|3 tbsp boiling water to the caramel mixture, which will splutter and spit. Add the butter and tilt the pan to mix the ingredients together. Leave to cool for 5 minutes.

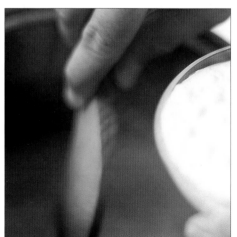

4 Gradually stir in the cream and mix well until thoroughly combined. Pour into a jug (pitcher) and serve warm or cool.

Melba sauce

Of all the classic ice cream sauces, this is perhaps the best known. It is very easy, requires no cooking and is delicious served with scoops of vanilla ice cream and sliced ripe peaches. Some versions of this sauce are cooked and thickened with cornflour (cornstarch), but this simple version is by far the best.

MAKES 200ml | 7fl oz | scant 1 cup

INGREDIENTS

250g|9oz|1⅓ cups fresh or thawed frozen RASPBERRIES

30ml|2 tbsp ICING (CONFECTIONERS') SUGAR

1 Purée the raspberries in a food processor or blender until smooth.

Apricot Sauce

Delicious with vanilla ice cream, this fruity sauce is a good way of persuading children to eat fruit without realizing they are doing so.

MAKES 350ml | 12fl oz | 1½ cups

INGREDIENTS

200g|7oz|scant 1 cup DRIED APRICOTS

450ml|¾ pint|scant 2 cups WATER

25g|1oz\2 tbsp CASTER (SUPERFINE) SUGAR

VARIATION *The apricots can also be poached in apple juice or a mixture of half apple juice and half water.*

Combining sauces

Spoon a little Melba sauce over half a serving plate, then spoon apricot sauce over the other half. Tilt the plate very gently, first in one direction, then the other, to swirl the edges of the sauce together. Add the ice cream and decorate with sprigs of mint.

2 Pour the purée into a sieve (strainer) set over a bowl. Press the fruit through the sieve and discard the seeds that remain behind in the sieve. Sift in the icing sugar, stir the mixture until smooth and chill until required.

1 Put the dried apricots in a pan and add the water and sugar. Cover and leave to simmer for 10 minutes until the apricots are tender and plump. Leave to cool.

This is a wonderful way of using up ripe raspberries. If they are particularly soft, don't purée them first; check them over, then simply press through a sieve (strainer) with the aid of a wooden spoon.

2 Tip the mixture into a blender or food processor and process to a smooth purée. Scrape into a bowl and chill until ready to serve.

INSTANT DESSERTS

Serving plain ice cream with a combination of sauces is a very quick and easy way to produce an exciting dessert. Sauces that contrast in colour or texture are very attractive when used together, but avoid using flavours that are not complementary.

COOK'S TIP *Sauces that contrast with each other can be rippled or swirled in exactly the same way as rippling ice cream. Ice cream is then placed on the top.*

Decorations

Complete the simplest dish of beautifully scooped ice cream or a party-style sundae with one of these professional looking decorations and you will be sure to impress your dinner guests.

How to make decorations

Plain chocolate caraque

1 Using a spatula or the back of a spoon spread melted dark (bittersweet) chocolate over a marble slab or cheese board, to a depth of 5mm|¼in. Leave in a cool place to cool and harden.

Two-tone caraque

2 Draw a long, fine-bladed cook's knife across the chocolate at a 45° angle, using a see-saw action to pare away long curls. If the chocolate is too soft, put it in the refrigerator for 5 minutes or in a cold place for 15 minutes.

Piped chocolate shapes

Spoon some melted dark (bittersweet) chocolate into a paper piping (pastry) bag and snip off the tip. Pipe squiggly shapes, hearts, butterflies, or even initials on to a lined baking sheet. Peel off when cool and chill until required.

1 Spoon alternate lines of melted white and dark (bittersweet) chocolate over a marble slab or cheese board, and spread lightly so that all the chocolate is the same height. Leave the chocolate to cool and harden.

2 Pare away long, thin curls of chocolate with a fine-bladed cook's knife in the same way that you do when making plain (semisweet) chocolate caraque.

Chocolate rose leaves

Brush melted dark (bittersweet) chocolate, as evenly as possible, over the underside of clean, dry rose leaves. Avoid brushing over the edges. Put the leaves on to a baking parchment-lined baking sheet and leave in a cool place to set. Carefully peel each leaf away and chill until they are required.

Simple chocolate curls

Holding a bar of dark (bittersweet), white or milk chocolate over a plate, pare curls away from the edge, using a swivel-blade vegetable peeler. Lift the pared curls carefully with a flat blade or a slim spatula and arrange as desired.

COOK'S TIP *If the chocolate used for decoration is not at the right temperature the curls will either be too brittle or won't hold their shape. Set the chocolate aside at room temperature for 20 minutes before working with it.*

How to make dipped fruits

Fruit both looks and tastes fabulous when it is half dipped in melted dark (bittersweet) or white chocolate. Choose from tiny strawberries (still with their green hulls attached), little clusters of green or red grapes, physalis or cherries, with their stalks. It can also look very effective if you dip half the fruits in dark chocolate and the remainder in white chocolate. Once they have been dipped, leave the fruits to set on a large baking sheet lined with baking parchment.

Caramel-dipped fruits

For a more unusual fruit decoration for ice cream dishes, half-dip peeled physalis, whole strawberries or cherries (with the stalks intact) into warm caramel, then leave to cool and harden on an oiled baking sheet.

COOK'S TIP *Always carefully select fruit used for decoration and check that the fruit is perfect and free of any bruising as this will quickly spoil the decoration. Wipe them over with a damp cloth to remove any dust. A more even effect can be achieved if the stalks are still firmly attached to the fruit.*

Caramel shapes

The caramel used for making baskets is also suitable for making fancy shapes to decorate ice cream sundaes. Instead of drizzling the caramel on to foil-covered oranges, drizzle shapes such as treble clefs, graduated zigzags, spirals, curly scribbles, initials, stars or hearts on to a lightly oiled baking sheet. Vary the sizes, from small decorations about 5cm|2in long to larger 10cm|4in long shapes.

Using coloured chocolate

1 Pipe random lines of melted dark (bittersweet) chocolate over a piece of baking parchment. Overpipe with piped white chocolate. Using pink liquid food colouring, tint a little of the melted white chocolate.

2 Pipe a third layer of chocolate squiggles, this time in pink, over the dark and white layers. Chill in the refrigerator until set.

3 Break the coloured shapes into jagged fragments of varying sizes and stick them into ice cream to decorate. They look particularly good on top of ice cream sundaes.

Frosted flowers

1 Lightly beat an egg white, then brush a very thin layer over edible flowers such as pansies, violas, nasturtiums, tiny rose buds or petals. Herb flowers can also be used, as can strawberries, seedless grapes or cherries.

2 Sprinkle the flower or fruit liberally with caster (superfine) sugar and leave to dry on a large plate or wire cooling rack. Use on the day of making and handle with care as the flowers will be brittle and delicate.

Meringue dainties

1 Make a meringue mixture using 2 egg whites and 115g|4oz|generous ½ cup caster (superfine) sugar. Spoon it into a large piping bag fitted with aplain 5mm|¼in or a 9mm|⅜in nozzle.

Citrus curls

1 Using a cannelle knife (zester), pare the rind of an orange, lemon or lime, removing just the coloured rind of the skin and leaving the bitter white pith on the fruit.

2 Dust the citrus curls with a little caster (superfine) sugar and use them to sprinkle over citrus-based ices such as lemon sorbet. Use on the day of making or store in an airtight container until needed.

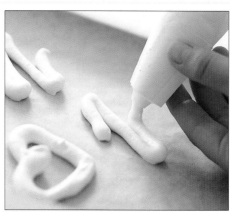

2 Pipe heart shapes, zigzags, shooting stars or geometric shapes on to baking sheets lined with baking parchment.

Corkscrews

1 Use a cannelle knife (zester) to pare long strips of orange, lemon or lime rind. The strips should be as long as possible and very narrow.

2 Twist the strips of rind tightly around cocktail sticks (toothpicks) so that they curl into corkscrews. Carefully slide the sticks out of the corkscrews and hang the curls over the edge of ice cream dishes.

3 Sprinkle the shapes lightly with caster sugar and bake at low heat until they are firm enough to be lifted off the paper easily. Cool, then store in an airtight container for up to 1 week.

Decorative effects with sauces

Spooning sauces over ice cream is a quick and simple method of decorating iced desserts, and this informal technique can look particularly pretty over ice cream sundaes. For a more elegant finish, sauces can also be piped in decorative shapes and patterns on scoops of ice cream, or used to create elaborate or dramatic backdrops on the surface of the dishes on which the ice cream is going to be served. These simple techniques are surprisingly quick and easy to use, and provide the perfect setting for home-made iced desserts.

Creating teardrops

1 Spoon a little Melba sauce over the base of a plate, tilt to cover, then pipe or spoon small dots of unwhipped double (heavy) cream around the edge of the plate.

2 Draw a skewer or cocktail stick (toothpick) through the dots to form teardrops. Scoop the ice cream into the centre of the plate.

Feathering

1 Spoon a little chocolate or butterscotch sauce over the base of a plate, then pipe a central dot and one or more circles of melted white chocolate or double (heavy) cream on the sauce, starting at the centre and working outwards.

2 Draw a skewer or cocktail stick (toothpick) in lines radiating out from the centre of the plate to the rim, like the spokes of a wheel. Alternatively, you could mark lines in alternate directions for a spider's web effect.

Piping zigzag lines

Arrange scoops of ice cream on a plate. Spoon cooled chocolate sauce into a greaseproof (waxed) paper piping (pastry) bag, snip off the tip, and pipe zigzags over the plate and ice cream. For added effect, dust with sifted cocoa.

Piped border

1 Pipe a swirly border of sieved (strained) strawberry or apricot jam around the edge of a plate. Alternatively, use melted white or dark (bittersweet) chocolate and leave to set.

2 Using the jam or chocolate as a border, flood the centre of the design with fruit, chocolate or butterscotch sauce, or cream. Arrange the ice cream on top, keeping it within the border.

Decorative squiggles

Spoon a little butterscotch or chocolate sauce over the base of a flat plate and tilt the plate to completely coat. Spoon melted white chocolate into a paper piping (pastry) bag, snip off the tip and pipe squiggly lines over the sauce. Leave to set, then arrange the ice cream.

the recipes

This section contains over 86 recipes for the exquisite desserts your ice cream machine was made for. Beautifully presented with easy-to-follow steps, recipes range from the classic flavours in ice creams and sorbets to healthy low-fat and low-sugar ices and impressive dinner-party desserts. With many different new and exciting flavours and combinations, every recipe will bring certain success.

classic sorbets& water ices

After a rich main course, nothing refreshes the palate better than a clean-tasting sorbet or water ice. Stock up the freezer when fruits are plentiful. The recipes containing raw egg white should be avoided by those who are susceptible to infections, such as the very young and the elderly, but the rest can be enjoyed by all.

Lemon Sorbet

This is probably the most classic sorbet of all. Refreshingly tangy and yet deliciously smooth, it quite literally melts in the mouth and is even more delicious topped with fresh summer berries.

SERVES SIX

INGREDIENTS

200g|7oz|1 cup
CASTER (SUPERFINE) SUGAR

300ml|½ pint|1¼ cups WATER

4 LEMONS, well scrubbed

1 EGG WHITE

SUGARED LEMON RIND,
to decorate

1 Put the sugar and water into a pan and bring to the boil, stirring occasionally until the sugar has just dissolved.

2 Using a swivel-blade vegetable peeler pare the rind thinly from two of the lemons so that it falls straight into the pan.

3 Simmer for 2 minutes without stirring, then take the pan off the heat. Leave to cool, then chill.

4 Squeeze the juice from all the lemons and add it to the syrup. Strain into a jug (pitcher) and chill before churning in an ice cream maker until thick.

5 Add the egg white and continue to churn for 10–15 minutes until firm enough to scoop.

6 Scoop into bowls or glasses and decorate with sugared lemon rind.

COOK'S TIP *Cut one third off the top of a lemon and retain as a lid. Squeeze the juice out of the larger portion. Remove any membrane and use the shell as a ready-made container. Scoop or pipe sorbet into the shell, top with lid and add lemon leaves or small bay leaves. Serve on a bed of crushed ice allowing one lemon per person.*

VARIATION *Sorbet can be made from any citrus fruit. As a guide you will need 300ml|½ pint|1¼ cups fresh fruit juice and the pared rind of half the squeezed fruits. Use 4 oranges or 2 oranges and 2 lemons, or, for a grapefruit sorbet, use the rind of one ruby grapefruit and the juice of two. For lime sorbet, combine the rind of three limes with the juice of six.*

Pear and Sauternes Sorbet

Based on a traditional sorbet that would have been served between savoury courses in France, this fruity ice is delicately flavoured with the honey bouquet of Sauternes wine and is spiked with brandy for an extra kick.

SERVES SIX

INGREDIENTS

675g|1½lb RIPE PEARS

50g|2oz|¼ cup CASTER (SUPERFINE) SUGAR

250ml|8fl oz|1 cup WATER plus 60ML|4 tbsp extra

250ml|8fl oz|1 cup SAUTERNES WINE, plus extra to serve

30ml|2 tbsp BRANDY

juice of ½ LEMON

1 EGG WHITE

FRESH MINT SPRIGS, dusted with icing (confectioners') sugar, to decorate

1 Quarter the pears, peel them and cut out the cores. Slice them into a pan and add the sugar and 60ml| 4 tbsp of the measured water. Cover and simmer for 10 minutes, or until the pears are just tender.

2 Tip the pear mixture into a food processor or blender and process until smooth, then scrape into a bowl. Leave to cool, then chill.

3 Stir the wine, brandy and lemon juice into the chilled pear purée with the remaining water. Churn the mixture in an ice cream maker until thick.

4 Lightly whisk the egg white with a fork until just frothy. Add to the sorbet in the ice cream maker and churn for 10 minutes more.

5 Serve the sorbet in small dessert glasses, with a little extra Sauternes poured over each portion. Decorate with the sugared mint sprigs.

COOK'S TIP *Sorbets that contain alcohol tend to take a long time to freeze, especially when made in an ice cream maker. To save time, transfer it to a tub as soon as it thickens and finish freezing it in the freezer.*

Red Berry Sorbet

This vibrant red sorbet seems to capture the true flavour of summer. Pick your own berries, if you can, and use them as soon as possible.

SERVES SIX

INGREDIENTS

150g|5oz|¾ cup CASTER (SUPERFINE) SUGAR

200ml|7fl oz|scant 1 cup WATER

500g|1¼lb|5 cups MIXED RIPE BERRIES, hulled, including two or more of the following: STRAWBERRIES, RASPBERRIES, TAYBERRIES or LOGANBERRIES

JUICE OF ½ LEMON

1 EGG WHITE

small whole and halved STRAWBERRIES and STRAWBERRY LEAVES AND FLOWERS, to decorate

1 Put the sugar and water into a pan and bring to the boil, stirring until the sugar has dissolved. Pour the syrup into a bowl, leave to cool, then chill.

2 Purée the fruits in a food processor or blender, then press through a sieve (strainer) into a large bowl. Stir in the syrup and lemon juice.

3 Churn in an ice cream maker until thick, then add the whisked egg white. Continue to churn until firm enough to scoop.

4 Scoop on to plates or bowls, and decorate with fresh strawberries, leaves and flowers.

VARIATION *For a fruity sorbet with a hidden kick, add 45ml|3 tbsp vodka or cassis to the fruit purée. Don't be too generous with the spirits or the sorbet will not freeze firmly.*

Blackcurrant Sorbet

Wonderfully sharp and bursting with flavour, this is a very popular sorbet. If you find it a bit tart, add a little more sugar before freezing.

SERVES SIX

INGREDIENTS

500g|1¼lb|5 cups BLACKCURRANTS, trimmed

350ml|12fl oz|1½ cups WATER

150g|5oz|¾ cup CASTER (SUPERFINE) SUGAR

1 EGG WHITE

SPRIGS OF BLACKCURRANTS, to decorate

1 Put the blackcurrants in a pan and add 150ml|¼ pint|⅔ cup of the measured water.

2 Cover the pan and simmer for 5 minutes or until the fruit is soft. Cool slightly, then purée in a food processor or blender.

3 Set a large sieve (strainer) over a bowl, pour the purée into the sieve then press it through the mesh with the back of a wooden spoon into the bowl below.

4 Pour the remaining measured water into the clean pan. Add the sugar and bring to the boil, stirring until the sugar has dissolved. Pour the syrup into a bowl. Cool, then chill. Mix the blackcurrant purée and sugar syrup together.

5 Churn in an ice cream maker until thick. Add the egg white and continue churning until it is firm enough to scoop.

6 Serve decorated with the blackcurrant sprigs.

Raspberry Sorbet

Sweet and silky smooth, sorbet is a good way of bringing out the flavour of slightly tart raspberries.

It's delicious served on its own or mixed with other sorbet flavours.

SERVES SIX

INGREDIENTS

150g|5oz|¾ cup CASTER (SUPERFINE) SUGAR

200ml|7fl oz|scant 1 cup WATER

500g|1¼lb|3 cups RASPBERRIES

juice of ½ LEMON

1 EGG WHITE

FRESH RASPBERRIES, to decorate

1 Put the sugar and water in a pan and bring to the boil, stirring until the sugar has dissolved. Pour into a bowl, leave to cool, then chill.

2 Purée the raspberries in a food processor or blender until smooth. Press the purée through a sieve into a large bowl. Stir in the syrup and lemon juice.

3 Pour the mixture into the ice cream maker and churn until thick. Lightly whisk the egg white and add to the machine. Continue to churn until firm enough to scoop.

4 Scoop the sorbet into bowls and decorate with fresh raspberries or turn into a freezer container and freeze until required.

Candied Clementine Sorbet

Clementines can usually be relied on at any time of the year for making a sweet, tangy juice that's full of

flavour. Use them in this refreshing sorbet that's specked with pieces of candied fruit.

SERVES SIX

INGREDIENTS

800g|1¾ lb CLEMENTINES

600ml|1 pint|2½ cups WATER

200g|7oz|1 cup CASTER (SUPERFINE) SUGAR

1 EGG WHITE

1 Cut half the clementines into quarters, discarding the stalk ends. Squeeze the juice from the remainder. Bring half the water to the boil in a heavy-based pan.

2 Add the clementines, cover and cook gently for 15 minutes to soften the skins. Stir in the sugar and heat gently until the sugar has dissolved.

3 Simmer very gently, uncovered, for about 45 minutes until the clementines are very tender and the liquid has reduced to a thick syrup.

4 Lift out the clementines with a fork and stir the remaining water into the syrup left in the pan.

COOK'S TIP *The candied strips can be wrapped in clear film (plastic wrap) and stored in the refrigerator for up to a week.*

5 When the clementines are cool, scrape the pulp away from six of the wedges and finely shred the skin. Reserve for decoration.

6 Chop the remaining wedges into small pieces in a food processor or blender using the pulse setting.

7 Pour the syrup from the pan, plus the squeezed juice into the ice cream maker and churn until thick. Whisk the egg white with a fork until broken up and add it to the ice cream maker with the chopped clementines. Churn for 2–3 minutes until thoroughly mixed.

8 Scoop into glasses and serve sprinkled with the shredded clementines, or transfer to a freezer container and freeze until ready to serve.

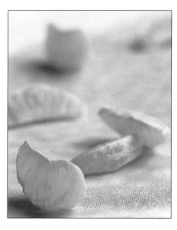

Strawberry and Lavender Sorbet

Delicately perfumed with just a hint of lavender, this delightful pastel pink sorbet is perfect

for a special-occasion dinner.

SERVES SIX

INGREDIENTS

150g|5oz|¾ cup CASTER (SUPERFINE) SUGAR

300ml|½ pint|1¼ cups WATER

6 FRESH LAVENDER FLOWERS, plus extra to decorate

500g|1¼lb|5 cups STRAWBERRIES, HULLED

1 EGG WHITE

1 Bring the sugar and water to the boil in a large pan, stirring until the sugar has dissolved.

2 Take the pan off the heat, add the lavender flowers and leave to infuse for 1 hour. Chill the syrup before using.

3 Purée the strawberries in a food processor or in batches in a blender, then press the purée through a large sieve (strainer) into a bowl.

4 Pour the strawberry purée into the bowl and strain in the lavender syrup. Churn until thick. Add the whisked egg white to the ice cream maker and continue to churn until the sorbet is firm enough to scoop.

5 Serve in scoops, piled into tall glasses, and decorate with sprigs of lavender flowers.

COOK'S TIP *The size of the lavender flowers can vary; if they are very small you may need to use eight. To double check, taste a little of the cooled lavender syrup. If you think the flavour is a little mild, add 2–3 more flowers, reheat and cool again before using.*

Minted Earl Grey Sorbet

Originally favoured by the Georgians at grand summer balls, this refreshing, slightly tart sorbet is perfect for a lazy afternoon in the garden.

SERVES SIX

INGREDIENTS

200g|7oz|1 cup CASTER (SUPERFINE) SUGAR

300ml|½ pint|1¼ cups WATER

1 LEMON, well scrubbed

45ml|3 tbsp EARL GREY TEA LEAVES

450ml|¾ pint|2 cups BOILING WATER

1 EGG WHITE

30ml|2 tbsp chopped fresh MINT LEAVES

FRESH MINT SPRIGS OR FROSTED MINT, to decorate

1 Put the sugar and water into a pan and bring the mixture to the boil, stirring until the sugar has completely dissolved.

2 Thinly pare the rind from the lemon so that it falls straight into the pan of syrup. Simmer for 2 minutes then pour into a bowl. Cool, then chill.

3 Put the tea into a pan and pour on the boiling water. Cover and leave to stand for 5 minutes, then strain into a bowl. Cool, then chill.

4 Remove the lemon rind from the syrup, add the tea and churn in an ice cream maker until thick.

5 Add the mint to the mixture. Lightly whisk the egg white until just frothy, then tip it into the ice cream maker and continue to churn until firm enough to scoop.

6 Serve in scoops, decorated with a few fresh or frosted mint leaves.

COOK'S TIP *If you only have Earl Grey tea bags these can be used instead, but add enough to make 450ml|¾ pint|scant 2 cups strong tea. Make frosted mint leaves by dipping the leaves in egg white and sprinkling them with caster (superfine) sugar.*

Sorbets on Sticks

Almost any firm-textured sorbet can be frozen in ice lolly moulds, making a convenient and "fun" presentation.

For summer entertaining, a splash of alcohol in the sorbet gives added appeal for adults,

but this can easily be omitted if an alcohol-free version is preferred.

MAKES ABOUT 24
DEPENDING ON THE SIZE
OF THE MOULDS

INGREDIENTS

**For the pineapple and
Kirsch lollies (popsicles)**

1 medium PINEAPPLE,
about 1.2kg|2½lb

115g|4oz|½ cup CASTER
(SUPERFINE) SUGAR

300ml|½ pint|1¼ cups WATER

30ml|2 tbsp LIME JUICE

60ml|4 tbsp KIRSCH

**For the pink grapefruit and
Campari lollies (popsicles)**

3 PINK GRAPEFRUIT, plus a little
extra GRAPEFRUIT or
ORANGE JUICE

115g|4oz|½ cup CASTER
(SUPERFINE) SUGAR

150ml|¼ pint|⅔ cup WATER

75ml|5 tbsp CAMPARI

1 For the pineapple lollies, slice the pineapple top and base, then cut away the skin. Cut the pineapple in half lengthways and cut away the core. Roughly chop the flesh and blend it in a food processor until smooth. Press the pulp through a sieve (strainer) placed over a bowl to extract as much juice as possible.

2 Heat the sugar and water in a heavy-based saucepan until the sugar dissolves. Bring to the boil and boil for 3 minutes, without stirring, to make a syrup. Remove from the heat and leave to cool. Stir in the lime juice and Kirsch.

3 Stir the pineapple juice into the syrup, then chill until very cold. Churn in an ice cream maker until the sorbet just holds its own shape but is not firm.

4 Spoon into 12 ice lolly moulds. Press a wooden lolly stick into the centre of each sorbet. Freeze overnight until firm.

5 To make the pink grapefruit and Campari lollies, cut away the skins from the grapefruit using a sharp knife. Slice the flesh, discarding any pips, and blend in a food processor until smooth, then press through a sieve placed over a bowl to extract as much juice as possible.

6 Measure the juice. You will need 450ml|¾ pint|scant 2 cups for the sorbet. If there is not enough, make it up with a little grapefruit or orange juice.

7 Heat the sugar and water in a heavy pan until the sugar has dissolved. Bring to the boil and boil for 3 minutes, without stirring, to make a syrup.

8 Leave to cool completely, then stir in the grapefruit juice and Campari. Chill until very cold.

9 Churn the mixture in an ice cream maker until the sorbet just holds its shape but is not firm. Spoon into 12 ice lolly moulds, position the sticks as in Step 4, and freeze overnight until firm.

10 To serve the lollies, dip the moulds in very hot water for 1–2 seconds, then carefully pull each lolly from the mould.

COOK'S TIP *Don't let the fact that you haven't any ice lolly (popsicle) moulds deter you from making this delicious dessert. Use wooden lolly sticks and make use of small plastic cups or even ice cube trays for miniature ice lollies.*

VARIATION *Other combinations that are just as delicious include orange sorbet with a dash of Cointreau, or lemon sorbet with gin. But don't be tempted to add too much alcohol or the sorbet will not freeze.*

VARIATION *Yellow-fleshed grapefruit can be used instead of ruby grapefruit.*

Damson Water Ice

Use ripe fruits to make the most of their natural sweetness. If you can't find damsons, use another

deep-red variety of plum or extra-juicy Victoria plums.

SERVES SIX

INGREDIENTS

500g|1¼lb RIPE DAMSONS, washed

450ml|¾ pint|scant 2 cups WATER

150g|5oz|⅔ cup CASTER
(SUPERFINE) SUGAR

1 Put the damsons into a pan and add 150ml|¼ pint|⅔ cup of the water. Cover and simmer for 10 minutes or until the damsons are tender.

2 Pour the remaining water into a second pan. Add the sugar and bring to the boil, stirring until the sugar has dissolved. Pour the syrup into a bowl, leave to cool, then chill.

3 Break up the cooked damsons in the pan with a wooden spoon and scoop out any free stones (pits). Pour the fruit and juices into a large sieve (strainer) set over a bowl. Press the fruit through the sieve and discard the skins and any remaining stones from the sieve.

4 Mix the damson purée with the syrup. Chill, then churn in an ice cream maker until firm enough to scoop.

5 Spoon into tall glasses or dishes and serve with wafers.

VARIATIONS *Apricot water ice can be made in the same way. Flavour the water ice with a little lemon or orange rind or add a broken cinnamon stick to the pan when poaching the fruit.*

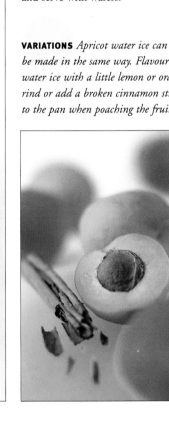

Apple and Cider Water Ice

This very English combination has a subtle apple flavour with just a hint of cider. As the apple purée is very pale, you could add a few drops of green food colouring to echo the pale green skin of the Granny Smith apples.

SERVES SIX

INGREDIENTS

500g|1¼lb GRANNY SMITH APPLES

150g|5oz|¾ cup CASTER (SUPERFINE) SUGAR

300ml|½ pint|1¼ cups WATER

250ml|8fl oz|1 cup STRONG DRY (HARD) CIDER

few drops of GREEN FOOD COLOURING (optional)

strips of thinly pared LIME RIND, to decorate

1 Quarter, core and roughly chop the apples. Put them into a pan. Add the sugar and half the water. Cover and simmer for 10 minutes, shaking the pan occasionally, until the apples are soft.

2 Press the mixture through a sieve (strainer) placed over a bowl. Discard the apple skins and seeds. Stir the cider and the remaining water into the apple purée and add a little colouring, if you like.

3 Chill, then churn in an ice cream maker until firm enough to scoop.

4 Scoop into dishes and decorate with twists of thinly pared lime rind.

COOK'S TIP *Add the food colouring gradually, making the mixture a little darker than you would like the finished sorbet to be, as freezing lightens the colour slightly.*

Rhubarb and Ginger Beer Sorbet

Rhubarb and ginger complement each other perfectly, and this pretty pastel-coloured sorbet packs a strong gingery punch. Serve with dainty ginger biscuits to heighten the ginger experience.

SERVES SIX

INGREDIENTS

500g|1¼lb|5 cups trimmed RHUBARB, washed and thickly sliced

350ml|12fl oz|1½ cups GINGER BEER

150g|5oz|¾ cup CASTER (SUPERFINE) SUGAR

few drops PINK FOOD COLOURING (optional)

1 EGG WHITE

To decorate

lightly poached and sweetened RHUBARB

strips of PRESERVED STEM GINGER

2 Put the remaining ginger beer into a pan with the sugar and bring to the boil, stirring until the sugar has completely dissolved. Pour the syrup into a bowl and leave to cool.

3 Pour the rhubarb and sugar syrup into an ice cream maker, mix in a few drops of pink food colouring, if using and churn until thick. Add the egg white and continue churning until firm enough to scoop.

4 Transfer to a freezer container and freeze until required.

5 Scoop into shallow bowls and serve decorated with the lightly poached rhubarb and strips of stem ginger.

COOK'S TIP *Try to use supple stems of young, forced rhubarb for this recipe as they have a more subtle flavour than the tougher stems of maincrop rhubarb.*

1 Put the rhubarb and 90ml|6 tbsp ginger beer into a pan, cover and cook gently until the rhubarb is tender and still bright pink. Cool slightly then purée until smooth.

Espresso Sorbet

The perfect finale for those guests who usually decline dessert. Light, refreshing, yet with the full mature depth of a strongly roasted cup of coffee. Serve with crisp biscuits, a drizzle of cream or spoonful of crème fraîche.

SERVES SIX

INGREDIENTS

90ml|6 tbsp good-quality
ESPRESSO GROUND
FILTER COFFEE

1 litre|1¾ pints|4 cups
boiling WATER

115g|4oz|½ cup LIGHT
MUSCOVADO (BROWN) SUGAR

1 EGG WHITE

dainty CHOCOLATE BISCUITS
(COOKIES), to serve

1 Spoon the coffee into a cafetière (press pot) or jug (pitcher), pour on 750ml|1¼ pints|3 cups of the boiling water and leave to stand for 5 minutes.

2 Pour the remaining boiling water into a pan, add the sugar and heat until all of the sugar has dissolved. You can test for this by checking a spoonful of the liquid. Once the sugar has dissolved, bring the mixture to the boil.

3 Simmer the sugar mixture for 2 minutes. Allow the liquid to cool slightly and then pour it into a large bowl.

COOK'S TIP *For a special occasion you could add a dash of coffee liqueur to the mixture before you churn it.*

4 Plunge the cafetière or strain the coffee from the jug. Pour the coffee into a the bowl containing the sugar syrup, leave to cool then chill well.

5 Once the coffee mixture is completely chilled, pour into an ice cream maker and churn until starting to thicken.

6 Add the egg white and continue churning until the mixture is firm enough to scoop.

7 Spoon into glasses or attractive espresso cups and serve at once with dainty chocolate biscuits, if liked. If you don't want to serve the sorbet immediately, transfer it to a freezer container and freeze until required.

classic
vanilla, chocolate & coffee ice creams

This chapter provides the best classic vanilla ice cream recipes plus some imaginative variations using ingredients such as brandied fruits, crumbled cookies, saffron and cinnamon. The principal flavours of chocolate, coffee and toffee ice cream are many people's favourites, making this selection the ultimate collection of everyday ice creams.

Classic Vanilla Ice Cream

Nothing beats the creamy simplicity of true vanilla ice cream. Vanilla pods are expensive, but they are well worth buying for the superb flavour they impart.

SERVES FOUR

INGREDIENTS

1 VANILLA POD (BEAN)

300ml|½ pint|1¼ cups SEMI-SKIMMED (LOW-FAT) MILK

4 EGG YOLKS

75g|3oz|6 tbsp CASTER (SUPERFINE) SUGAR

5ml|1 tsp CORNFLOUR (CORNSTARCH)

300ml|½ pint|1¼ cups DOUBLE (HEAVY) CREAM

1 Slit the vanilla pod lengthways. Pour the milk into a heavy pan, add the vanilla pod and bring to the boil. Remove from the heat and leave to infuse for 15 minutes.

2 Lift the vanilla pod up. Holding it over the pan, scrape the black seeds out of the pod into the milk.

3 Set the vanilla pod aside and bring the milk back to the boil.

4 Whisk the egg yolks, sugar and cornflour in a bowl until thick and foamy. Gradually pour on the hot milk, whisking constantly. Return to the pan and cook over a gentle heat, stirring all the time.

5 When the custard thickens and is smooth, pour it back into the bowl. Cool it, then chill.

6 Whip the cream until it has thickened but still falls from a spoon. Stir the cream into the custard and churn the mixture in an ice cream maker until thick.

7 Scoop the ice cream into dishes, bowls or cones – or eat straight from the tub.

COOK'S TIP *Don't throw the vanilla pod (bean) away after use. Instead, rinse it in cold water, dry and store in the sugar jar. After a week or so the sugar will take on the wonderful aroma and flavour of the vanilla and will be delicious sprinkled over summer fruits. Use it to sweeten whipped cream, custard, cookies and shortbread.*

Brown Bread Ice Cream

This very English ice cream consists of creamy vanilla ice cream flecked with tiny clusters of crisp,

crunchy caramelized brown breadcrumbs and tastes similar to cookies-and-cream ice cream.

SERVES FOUR TO SIX

INGREDIENTS

4 EGG YOLKS

75g|3oz|6 tbsp CASTER (SUPERFINE) SUGAR

5ml|1 tsp CORNFLOUR (CORNSTARCH)

300ml|½ pint|1¼ cups SEMI-SKIMMED (LOW-FAT) MILK

40g|1½oz|3 tbsp BUTTER

75g|3oz|1½ cups FRESH BROWN BREADCRUMBS

50g|2oz|¼ cup LIGHT MUSCOVADO (BROWN) SUGAR

5ml|1 tsp VANILLA ESSENCE (EXTRACT)

300ml|½ pint|1¼ cups DOUBLE (HEAVY) CREAM

1 Whisk the egg yolks, sugar and cornflour together in a bowl until thick and pale. Bring the milk just to the boil in a heavy pan, then gradually pour it on to the egg yolk mixture, whisking constantly.

2 Return the mixture to the pan and cook over a gentle heat, stirring constantly until the custard thickens and is smooth. Pour it back into the bowl, leave to cool, then chill.

3 Melt the butter in a large frying pan. Add the breadcrumbs, stir until evenly coated in butter, then sprinkle the sugar over.

4 Fry gently for 4–5 minutes, stirring until lightly browned. Remove from the heat and leave until cool and crisp.

5 Add the vanilla essence to the custard and mix well. Stir in the cream. Transfer to an ice cream maker and churn until thick.

6 Rub the fried breadcrumbs between your fingers to break up any lumps.

7 Stir the breadcrumbs into the ice cream mixture, then churn for 5–10 minutes more until ready to serve in scoops.

COOK'S TIP *Watch the breadcrumbs carefully when frying. Like almonds, they have a habit of burning if you turn your back on them for a moment, and burnt crumbs will give the ice cream a bitter taste. The crumbs should darken only slightly.*

Crème Fraîche and Honey Ice Cream

This delicately flavoured vanilla ice cream is naturally sweetened with fragrant honey and is absolutely
delicious either on its own or with hot apple or cherry pie.

SERVES FOUR

INGREDIENTS

4 EGG YOLKS

60ml|4 tbsp CLEAR HONEY

5ml|1 tsp CORNFLOUR
(CORNSTARCH)

300ml|½ pint|1¼ cups
SEMI-SKIMMED
(LOW-FAT) MILK

7.5ml|1½ tsp VANILLA ESSENCE
(EXTRACT)

250g|9oz|generous 1 cup
CRÈME FRAÎCHE

NASTURTIUM, PANSY or HERB
FLOWERS, to decorate

1 Whisk the egg yolks, honey and cornflour in a bowl until thick and foamy. Bring the milk just to the boil in a heavy pan, then gradually pour on to the yolk mixture, whisking constantly.

2 Return to the pan and cook over a gentle heat, stirring all the time until the custard thickens.

3 Pour the honey custard into a jug (pitcher) and then chill until it is completely cold.

4 Stir the vanilla essence and crème fraîche into the custard mix, pour into an ice cream maker and churn until thick and firm enough to scoop.

5 Serve in glass dishes. Decorate with nasturtiums, pansies or edible herb flowers.

COOK'S TIP *Measure the honey carefully and use level spoonfuls; if you are over generous, the honey flavour will dominate and the ice cream will be too sweet.*

Tutti Frutti Ice Cream

This Italian ice cream takes its name from an expression meaning "all the fruits". Four fruits have been used here, but you can create your own blend of candied or glacé fruits, including exotics such as papaya or mango.

SERVES FOUR TO SIX

INGREDIENTS

300ml|½ pint|1¼ cups
SEMI-SKIMMED
(LOW-FAT) MILK

1 VANILLA POD (BEAN)

4 EGG YOLKS

75g|3oz|6 tbsp CASTER
(SUPERFINE) SUGAR

5ml|1 tsp CORNFLOUR
(CORNSTARCH)

300ml|½ pint|1¼ cups
WHIPPING CREAM

150g|5oz|⅔ cup
MULTICOLOURED GLACÉ
(CANDIED) CHERRIES

50g|2oz|⅓ cup
SLICED CANDIED LIME and
ORANGE PEEL

50g|2oz|⅓ cup
CANDIED PINEAPPLE

1 Pour the milk into a heavy pan. Using a small, sharp knife, slit the vanilla pod lengthways, add it to the pan and bring the milk to the boil. Immediately remove the pan from the heat and leave the milk for 15 minutes to allow the vanilla flavour to infuse.

2 Lift the vanilla pod up out of the milk. Holding it over the pan of infused milk, scrape out the small black seeds so that they fall into the pan. Bring the flavoured milk back to a gentle boil over a low heat.

3 Meanwhile, whisk the egg yolks, sugar and cornflour in a bowl until the mixture is thick and foamy. Gradually pour in the flavoured milk, whisking all the time.

4 Pour the custard mixture back into the pan. Cook over a gentle heat, stirring constantly until the custard thickens and is smooth. Pour it back into the bowl and cover. Cool, then chill.

5 Mix the thickened custard with the cream. There is no need to whip the cream first. Churn the custard and cream mixture in a food processor until it is thick.

6 Finely chop the glacé cherries, candied peel and pineapple and fold into the ice cream. Churn in the ice cream maker for 5–10 minutes or return to the freezer for 2–3 hours, until firm enough to scoop.

VARIATION *Steep the glacé (candied) fruits in a little Kirsch before adding.*

Cookies and Cream Ice Cream

This wickedly indulgent ice cream is a favourite in the USA. To make the result even more luxurious,

use freshly baked home-made cookies with large chunks of chocolate and nuts.

SERVES FOUR TO SIX

INGREDIENTS

4 EGG YOLKS

75g|3oz|6 tbsp CASTER
(SUPERFINE) SUGAR

5ml|1 tsp CORNFLOUR
(CORNSTARCH)

300ml|½ pint|1¼ cups
SEMI-SKIMMED
(LOW-FAT) MILK

5ml|1 tsp VANILLA ESSENCE
(EXTRACT)

300ml|½ pint|1¼ cups
WHIPPING CREAM

150g|5oz CHUNKY CHOCOLATE
AND HAZELNUT COOKIES,
crumbled into chunky pieces

1 Whisk the egg yolks, sugar and cornflour in a bowl until the mixture is thick and foamy. Pour the milk into a heavy pan, bring it just to the boil, then pour it on to the yolk mixture in the bowl, whisking constantly.

2 Return to the pan and cook over a gentle heat, stirring until the custard thickens and is smooth. Pour it back into the bowl and cover closely. Leave to cool, then chill.

COOK'S TIP *Experiment with different types of cookie to find the type that gives the best results.*

3 Stir the vanilla essence into the custard. Stir in the whipping cream and churn in an ice cream maker until thick.

4 Scrape the ice cream into a freezerproof container. Fold in the cookie chunks and freeze for 2–3 hours until firm.

Brandied Fruit and Rice Ice Cream

Based on a favourite Victorian rice ice cream, this rich dessert combines spicy rice pudding with a creamy egg custard flecked with brandy-soaked fruits. The mixture is then frozen until it is just firm enough to scoop.

SERVES FOUR TO SIX

INGREDIENTS

50g|2oz|⅓ cup READY-TO-EAT STONED (PITTED) PRUNES

50g|2oz|⅓ cup READY-TO-EAT DRIED APRICOTS

50g|2oz|¼ cup GLACÉ (CANDIED) CHERRIES

30ml|2 tbsp BRANDY

150ml|¼ pint|⅔ cup SINGLE (LIGHT) CREAM

For the rice mixture

40g|1½oz|generous ¼ cup SHORT GRAIN RICE

450ml|¾ pint|scant 2 cups FULL-CREAM (WHOLE) MILK

1 CINNAMON STICK, halved, plus extra CINNAMON STICKS, to decorate

4 CLOVES

For the custard

4 EGG YOLKS

75g|3oz|6 tbsp CASTER (SUPERFINE) SUGAR

5ml|1 tsp CORNFLOUR (CORNSTARCH)

300ml|½ pint|1¼ cups FULL-CREAM (WHOLE) MILK

1 Chop the prunes, apricots and glacé cherries finely and put them in a bowl. Pour over the brandy. Cover the bowl and leave the fruit to soak for 3 hours or overnight if possible.

2 Put the rice, milk and whole spices in a pan. Bring the mixture to the boil, then simmer gently for 30 minutes, stirring occasionally until most of the milk has been absorbed by the rice.

3 Lift out the spices and leave the rice to cool. Chill until required.

4 Whisk the egg yolks, sugar and cornflour in a bowl until thick and foamy. Heat the milk in a heavy pan, then gradually pour it on to the yolks, whisking constantly.

5 Pour back into the pan and cook over a gentle heat, stirring until the custard thickens. Leave to cool, then chill.

6 Mix the chilled custard, rice and cream together. Churn in an ice cream maker until thick.

7 Spoon the ice cream into a freezerproof container and fold in the fruits. Freeze for 2–3 hours until the ice cream is firm.

8 Serve the ice cream in scoops decorated with cinnamon sticks.

COOK'S TIP *As the brandy-soaked fruits are very soft, it is better to remove the ice cream from the ice cream maker, fold in the fruits and then freeze the mixture in a tub until firm enough to scoop, rather than adding the soaked fruits to the machine. This way, the fruits do not disintegrate and their colours are preserved.*

Chunky Coffee Bean and Kahlúa Ice Cream

A wonderful combination of creamy dark coffee with a hint of coffee liqueur, peppered with crunchy chocolate-covered coffee beans. The beans used here have been coated with white, dark and milk chocolate, but all dark chocolate-covered beans would work just as well.

SERVES SIX

INGREDIENTS

4 EGG YOLKS

75g|3oz|6 tbsp CASTER
(SUPERFINE) SUGAR

5ml|1 tsp CORNFLOUR
(CORNSTARCH)

300ml|½ pint|1¼ cups SEMI-
SKIMMED (LOW-FAT) MILK

30ml|2 tbsp instant COFFEE
GRANULES OR POWDER

300ml|½ pint|1¼ cups DOUBLE
(HEAVY) CREAM

120ml|4fl oz|½ cup KAHLÚA

115g|4oz assorted CHOCOLATE-
COVERED COFFEE BEANS

a little sifted COCOA POWDER
(UNSWEETENED), to decorate

1 Whisk the egg yolks, sugar and cornflour in a bowl until the mixture is thick and pale. Heat the milk in a pan then gradually whisk into the yolk mixture. Return the custard to the pan and cook over a gentle heat, stirring constantly so that it does not catch on the bottom and burn.

2 When the custard has thickened and is smooth, pour it back into the bowl and mix in the instant coffee granules or powder, stirring continuously until all of the coffee has completely dissolved. Cover the custard with clear film (plastic wrap) to prevent a skin from forming, leave to cool then chill well before churning.

3 Stir the cream and Kahlúa into the coffee custard then pour into an ice cream maker. Churn until thick. Roughly chop 75g|3oz of the chocolate-covered coffee beans, add to the ice cream and churn until firm enough to scoop. Transfer to a freezer container and freeze until required.

4 Scoop the ice cream into coffee cups and decorate with the remaining chocolate-covered coffee beans and a light dusting of cocoa powder.

Double White Chocolate Ice Cream

Crunchy chunks of white chocolate are a bonus in this delicious ice cream. Serve it scooped in waffle cones dipped in dark (bittersweet) chocolate, for a sensational treat.

SERVES EIGHT

INGREDIENTS

4 EGG YOLKS

75g|3oz|6 tbsp CASTER (SUPERFINE) SUGAR

5ml|1 tsp CORNFLOUR (CORNSTARCH)

300ml|½ pint|1¼ cups SEMI-SKIMMED (LOW-FAT) MILK

250g|9oz WHITE CHOCOLATE, chopped

10ml|2 tsp VANILLA ESSENCE (EXTRACT)

300ml|½ pint|1¼ cups WHIPPING CREAM

8 CHOCOLATE-DIPPED CONES, to serve

1 Whisk the egg yolks, sugar and cornflour in a bowl until the mixture is thick and foamy. Pour the milk into a heavy pan, bring it to the boil, then gradually pour the hot milk on to the yolk mixture, whisking constantly.

2 Return the custard mixture to the pan and cook over a gentle heat, stirring constantly until the custard thickens and is smooth. Pour the hot custard back into the same bowl.

3 Add 150g|5oz of the chopped white chocolate to the hot custard, with the vanilla essence. Gently stir until the chocolate has melted, leave to cool, then chill.

4 Stir the cream into the custard, then churn the mixture until thick. Add the remaining chocolate and churn for 5–10 minutes until firm. Serve in chocolate-dipped cones.

VARIATION *If you prefer, scoop the ice cream into glass dishes and decorate with white chocolate curls or extra diced chocolate. Ice cream served this way won't go quite as far, so will only serve 4–6.*

Classic Dark Chocolate Ice Cream

Rich, dark and wonderfully luxurious, this ice cream can be served solo or drizzled with warm chocolate sauce. If you are making it in advance, don't forget to soften the ice cream before serving so that the full flavour of the chocolate comes through.

SERVES FOUR TO SIX

INGREDIENTS

4 EGG YOLKS

75g|3oz|6 tbsp CASTER (SUPERFINE) SUGAR

5ml|1 tsp CORNFLOUR (CORNSTARCH)

300ml|½ pint|1¼ cups SEMI-SKIMMED (LOW-FAT) MILK

200g|7oz DARK (BITTERSWEET) CHOCOLATE

300ml|½ pint|1¼ cups WHIPPING CREAM

SHAVED CHOCOLATE, to decorate

1 Whisk the egg yolks, sugar and cornflour in a bowl until thick and foamy. Pour the milk into a pan, bring it just to the boil, then gradually whisk it into the yolk mixture.

2 Return the mixture to the pan and cook over a gentle heat, stirring constantly until the custard thickens and is smooth. Take the pan off the heat.

3 Break the chocolate into small pieces and stir into the hot custard until it has melted. Leave to cool, then chill.

4 Whip the cream, and mix with the cool chocolate custard.

5 Place in an ice cream maker and churn until firm enough to scoop. Serve the ice cream in scoops, decorated with chocolate shavings.

COOK'S TIP *For the best flavour use a good quality chocolate with at least 75 per cent cocoa solids, such as top-of-the-range Belgian dark (bittersweet) chocolate or cooking chocolate.*

Chocolate Double Mint Ice Cream

Full of body and flavour, this creamy, smooth ice cream combines the sophistication of dark chocolate with the satisfying coolness of fresh chopped mint. Crushed peppermints provide extra crunch, and this classic combination of flavours will be loved by children and adults alike.

SERVES FOUR

INGREDIENTS

4 EGG YOLKS

75g|3oz|6 tbsp CASTER (SUPERFINE) SUGAR

5ml|1 tsp CORNFLOUR (CORNSTARCH)

300ml|½ pint|1¼ cups SEMI-SKIMMED (LOW-FAT) MILK

200g|7oz DARK (BITTERSWEET) CHOCOLATE, broken into squares

40g|1½oz|¼ cup PEPPERMINTS

60ml|4 tbsp CHOPPED FRESH MINT

300ml|½ pint|1¼ cups WHIPPING CREAM

sprigs of FRESH MINT dusted with ICING (CONFECTIONERS') SUGAR, to decorate

1 Put the egg yolks, sugar and cornflour in a bowl and whisk until thick and foamy. Pour the milk into a heavy pan, bring to the boil, then gradually whisk it into the yolk mixture.

2 Scrape the mixture back into the pan and cook over a gentle heat, stirring constantly until the custard thickens and is smooth. Scrape it back into the bowl, add the chocolate, a little at a time, and stir until melted. Cool, then chill.

3 Put the peppermints in a strong plastic bag and crush them with a rolling pin. Stir them into the custard with the chopped mint.

4 Mix the custard and cream together and churn the mixture in an ice cream maker until firm enough to scoop.

5 Serve the ice cream in scoops and then decorate with mint sprigs dusted with sifted icing sugar.

COOK'S TIP *If you freeze the ice cream in a tub, don't beat it in a food processor when breaking up the ice crystals, or the crunchy texture of the crushed peppermints will be lost.*

Chocolate and Hazelnut Brittle Ice Cream

For nut lovers and chocoholics everywhere, this luxurious ice cream is the ultimate indulgence. Rich, smooth dark chocolate is combined with crisp little chunks of sweet hazelnut brittle that provide a satisfying contrast. For a change, use other types of nuts, such as almonds, walnuts or pecan nuts.

SERVES FOUR TO SIX

INGREDIENTS

4 EGG YOLKS

175g|6oz| scant 1 cup SUGAR

5ml|1 tsp CORNFLOUR (CORNSTARCH)

300ml|½ pint|1¼ cups SEMI-SKIMMED (LOW-FAT) MILK

150g|5oz DARK (BITTERSWEET) CHOCOLATE, broken into squares

115g|4oz|1 cup HAZELNUTS

60ml|4 tbsp WATER

300ml|½ pint|1¼ cups WHIPPING CREAM

1 Whisk the egg yolks, sugar and cornflour in a bowl until thick and foamy. Pour the milk into a pan, bring it just to the boil, then gradually whisk it into the yolk mixture.

2 Scrape the mixture back into the pan and cook over a gentle heat, stirring constantly, until the custard has thickened and is smooth.

3 Take the pan off the heat and stir the chocolate into the hot custard, a few squares at a time.

4 Cool, then chill. Brush a baking sheet with oil and set it aside.

5 Meanwhile put the hazelnuts, remaining sugar and measured water in a large, heavy frying pan.

6 Place over a gentle heat and heat without stirring until all the sugar has dissolved.

7 Increase the heat slightly and cook until the syrup surrounding the nuts has turned pale golden.

8 Quickly pour the mixture on to the oiled baking sheet and leave to stand at room temperature until the hazelnut brittle (praline) cools and hardens.

9 Pour the chocolate custard into the ice cream maker and add the cream. Churn for 25 minutes or until it is thick and firm enough to scoop.

10 Break the nut brittle into pieces. Reserve a few pieces for decoration and finely chop the rest.

11 Scrape the ice cream into a tub and stir in the nut brittle pieces. Freeze for 2–3 hours or until firm enough to scoop.

12 Scoop the ice cream on to plates or dishes and decorate with the reserved praline.

Classic Triple Chocolate Terrine

This variation on the popular Neapolitan layered ice cream is made with smooth dark,

milk and white chocolate. Serve it in slices, sandwiched between rectangular wafer biscuits

or in a pool of warm dark chocolate sauce.

SERVES EIGHT TO TEN

INGREDIENTS

6 EGG YOLKS

115g|4oz|½ cup CASTER
(SUPERFINE) SUGAR

5ml|1 tsp CORNFLOUR
(CORNSTARCH)

450ml|¾ pint|scant 2 cups
SEMI-SKIMMED
(LOW-FAT) MILK

115g|4oz DARK (BITTERSWEET)
CHOCOLATE, broken into squares

115g|4oz MILK CHOCOLATE,
broken into squares

115g|4oz WHITE CHOCOLATE,
broken into squares

2.5ml|½ tsp VANILLA ESSENCE
(EXTRACT)

450ml|¾ pint|scant 2 cups
WHIPPING CREAM

1 Whisk the egg yolks, sugar and cornflour until thick. Pour the milk into a heavy pan and bring it to the boil. Gradually pour it on to the yolk mixture, whisking constantly, then return the mixture to the pan and simmer, stirring constantly until the custard thickens and is smooth.

2 Divide the custard among three bowls. Add the dark chocolate to one, the milk chocolate to another and the white chocolate and vanilla essence to the third.

3 Stir with separate spoons until the chocolate has completely melted. Cool, then chill. Line a 25 x 7.5 x 7.5cm|10 x 3 x 3in terrine or large loaf tin (pan) with clear film (plastic wrap).

4 Stir a third of the cream into each bowl, then churn the custard mixture until thick.

5 Return the remaining bowls of flavoured custard and cream mixture to the refrigerator.

COOK'S TIP *Make sure each layer of ice cream is firm before adding another, or the layers may merge. The dark (bittersweet) chocolate layer may need to be softened at room temperature before spreading.*

6 Spoon the milk chocolate ice cream into the lined terrine or loaf tin, level the surface using the back of a spoon and freeze the ice cream until it is firm.

7 Churn the white chocolate ice cream in an ice cream maker until it is thick and smooth, then spoon it into the tin. Level the surface and freeze the ice cream until it is firm.

8 Finally, churn the dark chocolate ice cream and spread it in the tin to form the top layer, making sure the surface is smooth and level.

9 Cover the terrine with clear film, then freeze it overnight. To serve, remove the clear film cover, then invert on to a plate. Peel off the clear film and serve in slices.

Chunky Chocolate Ice Cream

This creamy milk chocolate ice cream, topped with delicious chunks of milk, dark and white chocolate,

will satisfy even the sweetest tooth and will be a hit with adults as well as children.

SERVES FOUR TO SIX

INGREDIENTS

4 EGG YOLKS

75g|3oz|6 tbsp CASTER
(SUPERFINE) SUGAR

5ml|1 tsp CORNFLOUR
(CORNSTARCH)

300ml|½ pint|1¼ cups
SEMI-SKIMMED (LOW-FAT) MILK

200g|7oz MILK CHOCOLATE

50g|2oz DARK (BITTERSWEET)
CHOCOLATE, plus extra,
to decorate

50g|2oz WHITE CHOCOLATE

300ml|½ pint|1¼ cups
WHIPPING CREAM

1 Whisk the egg yolks, caster sugar and cornflour in a bowl until the mixture is thick and foamy. Pour the milk into a large, heavy pan. Heat the milk and bring it just to the boil, then gradually pour it on to the egg yolk mixture, whisking constantly.

2 Return the custard mixture to the pan and cook over a gentle heat, stirring constantly with a wooden spoon until the custard thickens and is smooth.

3 Pour the custard back into the bowl. Break 150g|5oz of the milk chocolate into squares, stir these into the hot custard, then cover closely. Leave to cool, then chill.

4 Chop the remaining milk, dark and white chocolate finely and keep on one side.

5 Mix the chocolate custard and the whipping cream and churn the mixture in an ice cream maker for 25–30 minutes until thick.

6 Scoop the churned ice cream out of the machine and into a plastic tub. Fold in the pieces of chocolate and freeze for 2–3 hours until firm enough to scoop.

7 Scoop into glasses or bowls and decorate with more pieces of chopped chocolate.

COOK'S TIP *For maximum flavour, use good quality Belgian chocolate or your favourite chocolate bar; avoid using dark, milk or white cake covering.*

Chocolate Ripple Ice Cream

This creamy, dark chocolate ice cream, unevenly rippled with wonderful swirls of rich chocolate sauce, will stay deliciously soft even after freezing. Not that it will remain in the freezer for long!

SERVES FOUR TO SIX

INGREDIENTS

4 EGG YOLKS

75g|3oz|6 tbsp CASTER (SUPERFINE) SUGAR

5ml|1 tsp CORNFLOUR (CORNSTARCH)

300ml|½ pint|1¼ cups SEMI-SKIMMED (LOW-FAT) MILK

250g|9oz DARK (BITTERSWEET) CHOCOLATE, broken into squares

25g|1oz|2 tbsp BUTTER, diced

30ml|2 tbsp GOLDEN SYRUP or LIGHT CORN SYRUP

90ml|6 tbsp SINGLE CREAM or CREAM and MILK MIXED

300ml|½ pint|1¼ cups WHIPPING CREAM

ICE CREAM WAFERS, to serve

1 Whisk the egg yolks, sugar and cornflour until thick and frothy. Bring the milk just to the boil in a heavy pan, then gradually pour it on to the yolk mixture, whisking constantly. Return to the pan and simmer, stirring until the custard thickens and is smooth.

2 Pour the chocolate custard back into the bowl and stir in 150g|5oz of the chocolate, until melted. Cover the custard closely, leave it to cool, then chill.

3 Put the remaining chocolate into a pan and add the butter and syrup.

4 Heat gently, stirring, until the chocolate and butter have melted.

5 Stir in the single cream or cream and milk mixture. Heat gently, stirring, until smooth then leave the chocolate sauce to cool.

6 Stir the cream into the custard and churn in an ice cream maker for 20–25 minutes until thick.

7 Add alternate spoonfuls of ice cream and sauce to a 1.5 litre| 2½ pint|6 cup plastic container.

8 Marble the ice cream and chocolate sauce together by running a knife through the mixture.

9 Cover and freeze the ice cream for 5–6 hours until it is firm enough to scoop.

10 Serve in scoops in bowls, glasses or plates.

COOK'S TIP *For the ultimate indulgence make more chocolate sauce than is required in the recipe and spoon the extra over the top of the chocolate ripple ice cream.*

Choca Mocha Sherbet

This dark chocolate sherbet is a cross between a water ice and a light cream-free ice cream, and is ideal for chocoholics who are trying to count calories.

SERVES FOUR TO SIX

INGREDIENTS

600ml|1 pint|2½ cups
SEMI-SKIMMED (LOW-FAT) MILK

40g|1½oz|⅓ cup UNSWEETENED
COCOA POWDER

115g|4oz| ½ cup CASTER (SUPERFINE)
SUGAR

5ml|1 tsp INSTANT COFFEE
GRANULES

CHOCOLATE-COVERED RAISINS,
to decorate

1 Gently heat the milk in a medium pan. Meanwhile, put the cocoa in a small bowl.

2 Add a little of the hot milk to the cocoa and mix to a paste.

COOK'S TIP *Use good quality cocoa and don't overheat the milk mixture or the finished ice may taste bitter. If there are any lumps of cocoa in the milk, beat the mixture with a balloon whisk to remove them.*

3 Add the remaining milk to the cocoa mixture, stirring all the time, then pour the chocolate milk back into the pan. Bring to the boil, stirring continuously.

4 Take the pan off the heat and stir in the sugar and the coffee granules. Pour into a jug (pitcher), leave to cool, then chill well.

5 When it is chilled, churn the mixture in an ice cream maker until it is very thick.

6 Scoop the ice cream into dishes or onto plates. Sprinkle each portion with a few chocolate-covered raisins.

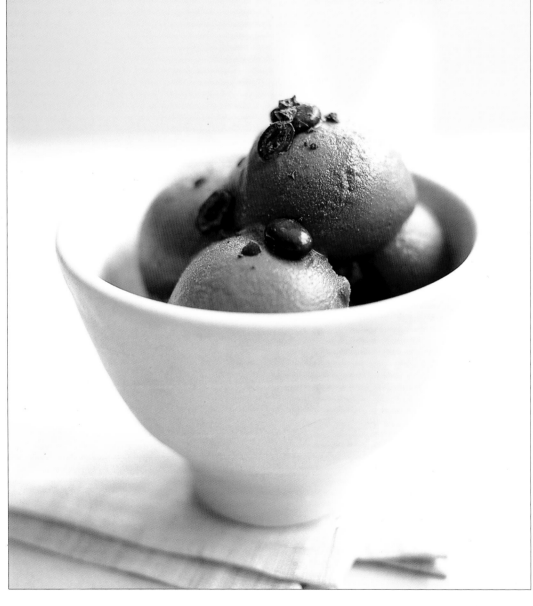

Iced Tiramisù

This favourite Italian combination makes a marvellous ice cream. Like the more traditional version, it tastes very rich, despite the fact that virtually fat-free fromage frais is a major ingredient.

SERVES FOUR

INGREDIENTS

150g|5oz|¾ cup CASTER (SUPERFINE) SUGAR

150ml|¼ pint|⅔ cup WATER

250g|9oz|generous 1 cup MASCARPONE

200g|7oz|scant 1 cup VIRTUALLY FAT-FREE FROMAGE FRAIS or CREAM CHEESE

5ml|1 tsp NATURAL VANILLA ESSENCE (EXTRACT)

10ml|2 tsp INSTANT COFFEE, dissolved in 30ml|2 tbsp BOILING WATER

30ml|2 tbsp COFFEE LIQUEUR

75g|3oz SPONGE FINGER BISCUITS (LADY FINGERS)

UNSWEETENED COCOA POWDER, for dusting

CHOCOLATE CURLS, to decorate

1 Put 115g|4oz|½ cup of the sugar into a small pan. Add the water and bring to the boil, stirring until the sugar has dissolved. Leave the syrup to cool, then chill it.

2 Put the mascarpone into a bowl. Beat it with a spoon until it is soft, then stir in the fromage frais. Add the chilled sugar syrup, a little at a time, then stir in the vanilla essence.

3 Spoon the mascarpone mixture into an ice cream maker and churn until it is thick but too soft to scoop.

COOK'S TIP *You can make chocolate curls from milk, dark (bittersweet) or white chocolate. Simply hold the bar of chocolate over a plate and pare curls away from the edge of the bar using a swivel-blade vegetable peeler. Lift the pared curls with a flat blade, a palette knife or a spatula rather than your fingers, and arrange as desired on top of the ice cream.*

4 Meanwhile, put the instant coffee mixture in a small bowl, sweeten with the remaining sugar, then add the liqueur. Stir well and leave to cool.

5 Crumble the sponge finger biscuits into small pieces and toss them in the coffee mixture.

6 Spoon a third of the ice cream into a 900ml|1½ pint|3¾ cup plastic container, spoon over half the biscuits then top with half the remaining ice cream.

7 Sprinkle over the last of the coffee-soaked biscuits, then cover with the remaining ice cream. Freeze for 2–3 hours until firm enough to scoop. Dust with cocoa powder and spoon into glass dishes. Decorate with chocolate curls, and serve.

Classic Coffee Ice Cream

This bittersweet blend is a must for those who like their coffee strong and dark with just a hint of cream. When serving, decorate with the chocolate-covered coffee beans that are available from some larger supermarkets and good confectioners.

4 Mix the coffee and cream with the chilled custard, then churn the mixture in an ice cream maker until firm enough to scoop.

5 Scoop the ice cream into glass dishes, sprinkle with chocolate-covered coffee beans and serve.

COOK'S TIP *If you only have coffee beans, put 50g|2oz|¼ cup in a mortar and crush with a pestle. Bring 300ml| ½ pint|1¼ cups semi-skimmed milk to the boil, and infuse (steep) the crushed beans for 15 minutes. Strain and use the flavoured milk to make the custard.*

SERVES FOUR TO SIX

INGREDIENTS

90ml|6 tbsp FINE FILTER COFFEE

250ml|8fl oz|1 cup BOILING WATER

4 EGG YOLKS

75g|3oz|6 tbsp CASTER (SUPERFINE) SUGAR

5ml|1 tsp CORNFLOUR (CORNSTARCH)

300ml|½ pint|1¼ cups SEMI-SKIMMED (LOW-FAT) MILK

150ml|¼ pint|⅔ cup DOUBLE (HEAVY) CREAM

1 Put the coffee in a cafetière (press pot) and pour on the boiling water. Leave to cool, then strain and chill until required.

2 Whisk the egg yolks, sugar and cornflour in a bowl until the mixture is thick and foamy. Pour the milk into a heavy pan, bring to the boil, then gradually pour on to the yolk mixture in the bowl, whisking constantly.

3 Return the mixture to the pan and cook over a gentle heat, stirring all the time until the custard thickens and is smooth. Pour it back into the bowl and cover closely with clear film (plastic wrap). Cool, then chill.

Coffee Toffee Swirl Ice Cream

A wonderful combination of creamy vanilla, marbled with coffee-flavoured toffee. Serve on its own as an impressive grand finale to a dinner party, or on a hot day as an ice cream sundae with classic coffee and chocolate ice cream.

SERVES FOUR TO SIX

INGREDIENTS

For the toffee sauce

10ml|2 tsp CORNFLOUR (CORNSTARCH)

170g|5¾oz can EVAPORATED MILK

75g|3oz|6 tbsp LIGHT MUSCOVADO (BROWN) SUGAR

20ml|4 tsp INSTANT COFFEE GRANULES

15ml|1 tbsp BOILING WATER

For the ice cream

4 EGG YOLKS

75g|3oz|6 tbsp CASTER (SUPERFINE) SUGAR

5ml|1 tsp CORNFLOUR (CORNSTARCH)

300ml|½ pint|1¼ cups SEMI-SKIMMED (LOW-FAT) MILK

5ml|1 tsp VANILLA ESSENCE (EXTRACT)

300ml|½ pint|1¼ cups WHIPPING CREAM

1 For the sauce, put the cornflour and a little evaporated milk in a small, heavy pan and mix to a smooth paste. Add the sugar and remaining evaporated milk.

2 Cook over a gentle heat, stirring until the sugar has dissolved, then increase the heat and cook, stirring continuously, until slightly thickened and just beginning to darken in colour.

3 Take the pan off the heat. Mix the coffee with the boiling water and stir into the sauce. Cool the sauce quickly by plunging the base of the pan into cold water.

4 Whisk the egg yolks, sugar and cornflour together until thick and foaming. Bring the milk just to the boil in a heavy pan then gradually whisk into the yolk mixture. Return to the pan and cook over a gentle heat, stirring until thick and smooth. Pour back into the bowl, stir in the vanilla and leave to cool.

5 Mix the custard and cream together and churn in an ice cream maker until thick but not firm enough to scoop. Transfer the semi-frozen churned ice cream to a plastic container.

6 Beat the toffee sauce well and drizzle it thickly over the ice cream. Marble the two together by roughly running a spoon through the mixture.

7 Cover and freeze the ice cream for 4–5 hours until it is firm enough to scoop. Serve in scoops in bowls or on plates.

COOK'S TIP *If the sauce is too thick to drizzle, gently warm the base of the pan for a few seconds, stirring well.*

VARIATION *The sauce is also delicious drizzled over plain vanilla ice cream.*

classic
fruit & nut
ice creams

From traditional fruit-flavoured ice creams to those speckled with chopped toasted nuts, this chapter imaginatively introduces the most widely used ice cream flavours. Fresh fruit purées, liqueured dried fruits and satisfying, crunchy nuts transform a basic ice cream into something very special.

Simple Strawberry Ice Cream

Capture the essence of childhood summers with this easy-to-make ice cream. Whipping cream is better than double cream for this recipe as it doesn't overwhelm the taste of the fresh fruit. Serve with extra strawberries or other summer fruits such as raspberries or redcurrants.

SERVES FOUR TO SIX

INGREDIENTS

500g|1¼lb|4 cups
STRAWBERRIES, hulled

50g|2oz|½ cup ICING
(CONFECTIONERS') SUGAR

juice of ½ LEMON

300ml|½ pint|1¼ cups
WHIPPING CREAM

extra STRAWBERRIES,
to decorate

1 Purée the strawberries in a food processor or blender until smooth, then add the icing sugar and lemon juice and process again. Press the purée through a sieve (strainer) into a bowl. Chill until very cold.

2 Churn the purée in an ice cream maker until mushy, then pour in the cream and churn until thick enough to scoop. Scoop into dishes and decorate with a few extra strawberries.

COOK'S TIP *If possible, taste the strawberries before buying them. Halve large strawberries for decoration.*

VARIATION *Raspberries or any other berries can be used to make this ice cream, in the same way as strawberries.*

Gooseberry and Clotted Cream Ice Cream

A rather neglected fruit, gooseberries can conjure up images of the tired grey-looking crumble that used to be served at school or in the work canteen. This indulgent ice cream puts gooseberries in a totally different class. Its delicious, slightly tart flavour goes particularly well with tiny, melt-in-the-mouth meringues.

SERVES FOUR TO SIX

INGREDIENTS

500g|1¼lb|4 cups
GOOSEBERRIES, trimmed

60ml|4 tbsp WATER

75g|3oz|6 tbsp CASTER
(SUPERFINE) SUGAR

150ml|¼ pint|⅔ cup
WHIPPING CREAM

a few drops of GREEN FOOD
COLOURING (optional)

120ml|4fl oz|½ cup
CLOTTED CREAM

FRESH MINT SPRIGS,
to decorate

MERINGUES, to serve

COOK'S TIP *Just a small amount of clotted cream adds a surprising richness to this simple ice cream. If the gooseberry purée is very tart, you can add extra sugar when mixing in the whipping cream.*

1 Put the gooseberries in a pan and add the water and sugar. Cover and simmer for 10 minutes or until soft. Tip into a food processor or blender and process to a smooth purée. Press through a sieve (strainer) placed over a bowl. Cool, then chill.

2 Mix the chilled purée with the whipping cream, add a few drops of green food colouring if using and churn in an ice cream maker until thickened and semi-frozen. Add the clotted cream and continue to churn until thick enough to scoop.

3 To serve, scoop the ice cream into dishes or small plates, decorate with fresh mint sprigs and add a few small meringues to each serving.

Blackberry Ice Cream

There could scarcely be fewer ingredients in this delicious, vibrant ice cream. If you make the ice cream in a machine, don't be tempted to add the cream with the fruit or the mixture will become buttery by the time it has been churned and is stiff enough to scoop.

SERVES FOUR TO SIX

INGREDIENTS

500g|1¼lb|5 cups BLACKBERRIES, hulled, plus extra, to decorate

75g|3oz|6 tbsp CASTER (SUPERFINE) SUGAR

30ml|2 tbsp WATER

300ml|½ pint|1¼ cups WHIPPING CREAM

CRISP DESSERT BISCUITS (COOKIES), to serve

1 Simmer the blackberries with the sugar and water until just soft. Tip the fruit into a sieve (strainer) placed over a bowl and press it through the mesh, using a wooden spoon. Leave to cool, then chill.

2 Churn the chilled purée in an ice cream maker for 10–15 minutes until it is thick, then gradually pour in the cream and continue to churn the ice cream until it is firm enough to scoop.

3 Scoop into dishes and decorate with extra blackberries. Serve with crisp dessert biscuits.

VARIATION *Frozen blackberries can be used for the purée. You will need to increase the cooking time to 10 minutes and stir occasionally. Blackcurrants can be used instead of blackberries. A combination of blackberries and peeled and sliced cooking apples also works well.*

Apricot and Amaretti Ice Cream

Prolong the very short season of fresh apricots by transforming them into this superb ice cream with crushed amaretti biscuits and whipped cream. If you want to make this ice cream when fresh apricots are not available, you can use the canned variety instead.

SERVES FOUR TO SIX

INGREDIENTS

500g|1¼lb FRESH APRICOTS, halved and stoned (pitted)

juice of 1 ORANGE

50g|2oz|¼ cup CASTER (SUPERFINE) SUGAR

300ml|½ pint|1¼ cups WHIPPING CREAM

50g|2oz AMARETTI

1 Put the apricots, orange juice and sugar in a heavy pan. Cover and simmer for 5 minutes until the fruit is tender. Leave the mixture to cool.

2 Lift out one-third of the fruit using a slotted spon and set it aside on a plate. Tip the remaining contents of the pan into a food processor or blender and process to a smooth purée.

3 Churn the apricot purée in an ice cream maker until the mixture is slushy, then gradually add the cream. Continue to churn until the ice cream is thick, but not firm enough to scoop.

4 Scrape the ice cream into a tub. Crumble the amaretti between your fingers so that the crumbs fall into the tub of ice cream.

5 Add the reserved apricots and gently fold them, and the amaretti crumbs, into the ice cream. Freeze for 2–3 hours until firm enough to scoop.

COOK'S TIP *It is better to chill the fruit purée if you have time, as this will speed up the churning or freezing process. If you have some amaretto liqueur, fold in 45ml\ 3 tbsp with the biscuits for an alcoholic kick.*

Banana and Toffee Ice Cream

Smooth and creamy condensed milk replaces the sugar in this fabulous ice cream. Because it's made without a cooked egg custard base, it's incredibly easy and fast.

SERVES FOUR TO SIX

INGREDIENTS

150g|5oz TOFFEES

3 RIPE BANANAS

juice of 1 LEMON

400g|14oz SWEETENED
CONDENSED MILK

450ml|¾ pint|scant 2 cups
WHIPPING CREAM

chopped TOFFEES, to decorate

COOK'S TIP *If making this ice cream for small children, you may prefer to use chopped chocolate instead of toffee.*

1 Unwrap the toffees and chop them as finely as possible, or if too firm to chop, put in a plastic bag and beat with a rolling pin or small hammer. (Make sure that the toffees are very finely crushed or they will make extremely hard lumps when they are frozen.)

2 Slice the bananas into a food processor, add the lemon juice and process until smooth. Pour in the condensed milk and process again to combine.

3 Mix the banana mixture with the cream and pour into the ice cream maker. Churn to a very soft scoop consistency and stir in the toffees.

4 Churn for 1–2 minutes to mix in. Transfer to a freezer container, cover and freeze for at least 2 hours before serving.

5 Scoop into bowls and serve scattered with extra toffees.

Rum and Raisin Ice Cream

For children this ice cream always seemed so much more sophisticated than mere vanilla. The longer you can leave the raisins to soak in the rum, the stronger the flavour will be.

SERVES FOUR TO SIX

INGREDIENTS

150g|5oz|scant 1 cup LARGE RAISINS

60ml|4 tbsp DARK RUM

4 EGG YOLKS

75g|3oz|6 tbsp LIGHT MUSCOVADO (BROWN) SUGAR

5ml|1 tsp CORNFLOUR (CORNSTARCH)

300ml|½ pint|1¼ cups SEMI-SKIMMED (LOW-FAT) MILK

300ml|½ pint|1¼ cups WHIPPING CREAM

DESSERT BISCUITS (COOKIES)

1 Put the raisins in a bowl, add the rum and mix together well. Cover the bowl and leave the raisins to soak for 3–4 hours or overnight.

2 Whisk the egg yolks, muscovado sugar and cornflour in a large bowl until the mixture is thick and foamy. Pour the milk into a heavy pan, and bring it to just below boiling point.

3 Gradually whisk the milk into the eggs, then pour the mixture back into the pan.

4 Cook over a gentle heat, stirring constantly until the custard thickens and is smooth. Take the pan off the heat and leave to cool.

5 Pour the cream into the custard, then churn until thick. Transfer to a plastic container.

6 Fold the soaked raisins into the ice cream, cover and freeze for 2–3 hours or until firm enough to scoop.

7 Serve in bowls or tall glasses with dessert biscuits.

COOK'S TIP *If you prefer, scoop the ice cream into cones. It will serve 6–8 people. If you haven't any dark rum, white rum, brandy or even whisky can be used instead.*

Mango and Passion Fruit Gelato

Fresh and fruity, this tropical ice cream has a delicate perfume and a delectable flavour and makes a refreshing dessert or snack during the hot summer months. Passion fruit tend to vary in size; if you can locate the large ones, four will be plenty for this dish.

2 Turn the slices inside out so that the pieces of mango stand proud of the skin, then scoop them into a food processor or blender, using a spoon. Finally, cut the remaining flesh away from the stones and add it to the rest.

3 Process the mango flesh until smooth, then add the grated lime rind, lime juice and caster sugar and process briefly.

4 Churn the fruit mixture in an ice cream maker for 10–15 minutes, then add the cream and continue to churn until the mixture is thick but still too soft to scoop. Scrape it into a plastic tub.

5 Cut the passion fruit in half and scoop the seeds and pulp into the ice cream mixture, mix well and freeze for 2 hours until firm enough to scoop.

SERVES FOUR

INGREDIENTS

4 LARGE MANGOES

grated rind and juice of 1 LIME

50g|2oz|¼ cup CASTER (SUPERFINE) SUGAR

300ml|½ pint|1¼ cups WHIPPING CREAM

4–6 PASSION FRUIT

1 Cut a thick slice from either side of the stone (pit) on each unpeeled mango. Using a sharp knife, make criss-cross cuts in the mango flesh, cutting down as far as the skin.

Apricot Parfait

Dried apricot purée adds a lively, fruity flavour to a creamy smooth ice cream, particularly when it is laced with orange liqueur. The caramelized sugar decoration isn't, of course, essential but it sets off the delicate colour of the ice cream.

SERVES SIX

INGREDIENTS

75g|3oz|scant 1 cup DEMERARA (RAW) SUGAR

200g|7oz|scant 1 cup DRIED APRICOTS

250ml|8fl oz|1 cup APPLE JUICE

60ml|4 tbsp COINTREAU or GRAND MARNIER

4 EGG YOLKS

75g|3oz|6 tbsp CASTER (SUPERFINE) SUGAR

5ml|1 tsp CORNFLOUR (CORNSTARCH)

300ml|½ pint|1¼ cups FULL CREAM (WHOLE) MILK

300ml|½ pint|1¼ cups DOUBLE (HEAVY) CREAM

grated rind and juice of ½ LEMON

1 Preheat the grill (broiler) to its lowest setting. Line a baking sheet with foil and mark six 10cm|4in circles on to the foil. Sprinkle the demerara sugar into the circles. Heat under the grill for about 3–4 minutes, watching closely, until the sugar has caramelized. Leave to cool.

2 Finely chop 50g|2oz|¼ cup of the apricots and reserve on one side. Roughly chop the remainder and put in a pan with the apple juice.

3 Simmer the apricots and apple juice for 10 minutes until the apricots are soft and plump. Leave to cool then blend until smooth and stir in the liqueur.

4 Whisk the egg yolks, sugar and cornflour in a bowl until light and frothy. Bring the milk just to the boil in a heavy pan. Pour the milk over the whisked mixture, whisking well to combine.

5 Pour the custard back into the pan and cook over a very gentle heat, stirring until slightly thickened. Pour into a bowl and leave to cool completely.

6 Stir the cream and apricot purée into the custard, pour into the ice cream maker and churn until thick. Tip in the chopped apricots and churn lightly to mix in. Turn into a freezer container and freeze until ready to serve.

7 Scoop the ice cream into small bowls. Break the caramelized sugar into chunky pieces and use to decorate.

COOK'S TIP *The sugared decorations will slowly soften if left exposed. If making them in advance, loosen them from the foil and cover with very lightly oiled clear film (plastic wrap). Store in a cool place.*

Pineapple Crush

Look out for pineapples that are labelled "extra sweet". This variety has bright sunflower-yellow flesh that is naturally sweet and juicy. It is ideal for making the most wonderful ice cream.

SERVES FOUR

INGREDIENTS

2 EXTRA-SWEET PINEAPPLES

300ml|½ pint|1¼ cups WHIPPING CREAM

50g|2oz|¼ cup CASTER (SUPERFINE) SUGAR

1 Slice one pineapple in half through the leafy top, then scoop out the flesh from both halves, keeping the shells intact. Drain them upside down, wrap in clear film (plastic wrap) and chill.

2 Trim the top off the remaining pineapple, cut the flesh into slices, then cut away the skin and any "eyes". Remove the core from each slice, then finely chop the flesh from both pineapples.

3 Purée 300g|11oz of the pineapple in a food processor or blender. Set aside the remaining chopped pineapple.

4 Churn the pineapple purée with the sugar for 15–20 minutes. Mix in the cream and churn until thick but still too soft to scoop.

5 Add the pineapple to the ice cream maker and continue to churn the ice cream until it is stiff enough to serve in scoops.

6 Serve the ice cream in scoops in the pineapple shells. Offer any remaining pineapple separately. Fold in 175g|6oz|1½ cups of the chopped pineapple and freeze for 2–3 hours before serving.

VARIATION *This ice cream is also delicious mixed with meringues: crumble four meringue nests into the ice cream mixture when adding the finely chopped pineapple.*

Peach and Cardamom Yogurt Ice

SERVES FOUR

The velvety texture of this smooth peach ice cream spiced with cardamom suggests it is made with cream, but the secret ingredient is actually natural yogurt; great for those watching their waistline.

INGREDIENTS

8 CARDAMOM PODS

6 PEACHES,
total weight about 500g|1¼lb, halved
and stoned (pitted)

75g|3oz|6 tbsp CASTER
(SUPERFINE) SUGAR

30ml|2 tbsp WATER

200ml|7fl oz|scant 1 cup
NATURAL (PLAIN) YOGURT

1 Crush the cardamom pods with the bottom of a ramekin.

2 Chop the peaches roughly and put them in a pan. Add the crushed cardamom pods, with their black seeds, and the sugar and water. Cover the pan and simmer for 10 minutes or until the fruit is tender. Leave to cool.

3 Tip the peach mixture into a food processor or blender, process until smooth, then press through a sieve (strainer) placed over a bowl.

4 Churn the purée in an ice cream machine until it is thick, then scrape it into a plastic tub and stir in the yogurt.

5 Freeze the purée and yogurt mixture until it is firm enough to scoop.

COOK'S TIP *Use bio natural (plain) yogurt for its extra mild taste. Ordinary natural yogurt is sharper and more acidic and tends to overwhelm the delicate taste of the peaches. You could use crème fraîche in place of the yogurt for a slightly richer, creamier flavour.*

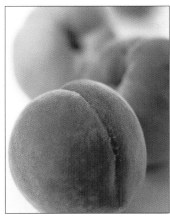

6 Using a melon baller, scoop on to a large platter and serve at once.

Rhubarb and Ginger Ice Cream

This "fruit" was so highly favoured by Queen Victoria that two varieties were grown and named after her and her consort Prince Albert. The classic combination of gently poached rhubarb and chopped ginger is brought up to date by blending it with mascarpone to make this pretty blush-pink ice cream.

SERVES FOUR TO SIX

INGREDIENTS

5 pieces of PRESERVED STEM GINGER

450g|1lb trimmed RHUBARB, sliced

115g|4oz|½ cup CASTER (SUPERFINE) SUGAR

30ml|2 tbsp WATER

150g|5oz|⅔ cup MASCARPONE

150ml|¼ pint|⅔ cup WHIPPING CREAM

WAFER CUPS, to serve (optional)

1 Using a sharp knife, roughly chop the stem ginger and set it aside. Put the rhubarb slices into a pan and add the sugar and water.

2 Cover and simmer for 5 minutes until the rhubarb is just tender and still bright pink.

3 Tip the mixture into a food processor or blender, process until smooth, then leave to cool. Chill if time permits.

4 Churn the rhubarb purée in an ice cream maker for 15–20 minutes until it is thick.

VARIATION *If the rhubarb purée is rather pale, add a few drops of pink food colouring when you put the mixture in the blender.*

5 Put the mascarpone into a bowl, soften it with a wooden spoon, then gradually beat in the cream.

6 Add the chopped ginger, then transfer to the ice cream maker and churn until firm. Serve as scoops in bowls or wafer baskets.

Nougat Ice Cream

Flavoured with traditional nougat ingredients – nuts, candied peel and orange flower water, this ice cream also imitates nougat in the way it's sandwiched between layers of rice paper. For convenience, let the ice cream freeze until firm, then cut it up and return to the freezer so it's ready to serve.

SERVES SIX

INGREDIENTS

50g|2oz|½ cup HAZELNUTS

50g|2oz|½ cup PISTACHIO NUTS

50g|2oz|⅓ cup CANDIED PEEL

4-6 sheets RICE PAPER

3 EGG YOLKS

30ml|2 tbsp ORANGE FLOWER WATER

75g|3oz|6 tbsp CASTER (SUPERFINE) SUGAR

5ml|1tsp CORNFLOUR (CORNSTARCH)

300ml|½ pint|1¼ cups FULL CREAM (WHOLE) MILK

300ml|½ pint|1¼ cups EXTRA THICK DOUBLE (HEAVY) CREAM

1 Spread out the hazelnuts on a baking sheet and brown them lightly under a hot grill (broiler). Mix with the pistachio nuts and roughly chop. Chop the candied peel.

2 Line the base and sides of a 28 x 18 x 4cm|11 x 7 x 1½in shallow baking tin (pan) with clear film (plastic wrap), then with a layer of rice paper, making sure you overlap the sheets slightly.

3 Whisk together the egg yolks, orange flower water, sugar and cornflour in a bowl until light and frothy. Bring the milk just to the boil in a heavy pan.

4 Pour the boiling milk over the yolk mixture, whisking together well to combine.

5 Pour the custard back into the pan and cook it over a very gentle heat, stirring continuously until the mixture has slightly thickened. Take off the heat.

6 Pour the custard back into the bowl, cover with a circle of baking parchment and leave to cool completely.

7 Stir in both types of cream, pour into the ice cream maker and churn until thick. Sprinkle in the nuts and churn again until just mixed. Spoon the ice cream into the paper-lined tin, spreading it in an even layer. Cover with another layer of rice paper. Freeze for at least 4 hours, or overnight, until firm.

8 To serve, invert the tin on to a board and remove the clear film. Cut the ice cream into squares or triangles, pile up on a plate and serve.

VARIATION *Use toasted blanched almonds instead of pistachios if you prefer. The meringue can be flavoured with rose water or grated lemon rind instead of orange flower water.*

Maple and Pecan Nut Ice Cream

This all-American ice cream is even more delicious when it is served with extra maple syrup and topped with whole pecan nuts.

SERVES FOUR TO SIX

INGREDIENTS

115g|4oz|1 cup PECAN NUTS

4 EGG YOLKS

50g|2oz|¼ cup CASTER
(SUPERFINE) SUGAR

5ml|1 tsp CORNFLOUR
(CORNSTARCH)

300ml|½ pint|1¼ cups
SEMI-SKIMMED (LOW-FAT) MILK

60ml|4 tbsp MAPLE SYRUP

300ml|½ pint|1¼ cups
WHIPPING CREAM

extra MAPLE SYRUP AND PECAN
NUTS, to serve

1 Cut the pecan nuts in half lengthways, spread them out on a baking sheet and grill (broil) them under a medium heat for 2–3 minutes until lightly browned. Remove the pecan nuts from the heat and leave to cool.

2 Place the egg yolks, sugar and cornflour in a bowl and whisk until thick and foamy. Pour the milk into a heavy pan, bring to the boil, then gradually whisk it into the yolk mixture.

3 Return the mixture to the pan and cook over a gentle heat, stirring constantly until the custard thickens and is smooth.

4 Pour the custard back into the bowl, and stir in the maple syrup.

5 Leave the mixture to cool in the bowl, then chill in the refrigerator until it is completely cold.

6 Stir the cream into the custard, then churn the mixture in an ice cream maker until thick. Scrape into a plastic container.

7 Fold in the nuts. Freeze for 2–3 hours until firm enough to scoop into dishes. Pour extra maple syrup over each portion and top with extra pecan nuts.

COOK'S TIP *Avoid "maple-flavoured" syrup, which can taste harsh and have a rather synthetic flavour. Look out for "pure maple syrup" on the label.*

Rocky Road Ice Cream

This American classic ice cream is a mouth-watering combination of roughly crushed nut brittle, rich vanilla custard and whipping cream.

SERVES FOUR TO SIX

INGREDIENTS

4 EGG YOLKS

5ml|1 tsp CORNFLOUR (CORNSTARCH)

225g|8oz|generous 1 cup SUGAR

300ml|½ pint|1¼ cups SEMI-SKIMMED (LOW-FAT) MILK

10ml|2 tsp VANILLA ESSENCE (EXTRACT)

OIL, for greasing

50g|2oz|½ cup MACADAMIA NUTS

50g|2oz|½ cup HAZELNUTS

50g|2oz|½ cup FLAKED (SLICED) ALMONDS

60ml|4 tbsp WATER

300ml|½ pint|1¼ cups WHIPPING CREAM

1 Put the egg yolks in a bowl and stir in the cornflour, with 75g| 3oz|6 tbsp of the sugar. Whisk until the mixture has turned thick and foamy.

2 Pour the milk into a heavy pan, bring it to the boil, then gradually whisk it into the yolk mixture in the bowl.

3 Return the mixture to the pan. Cook over a gentle heat, stirring constantly until the custard thickens and is smooth.

4 Pour it back into the bowl and stir in the vanilla essence. Leave to cool, then chill.

COOK'S TIP *If the nuts fail to brown evenly when you are making the nut brittle (praline) in the frying pan, don't stir the syrup. Instead, tilt the pan first one way then the other.*

5 Grease a large baking sheet with oil. Put the remaining sugar in a large, heavy frying pan, sprinkle the nuts on top and pour over the water.

6 Heat gently, without stirring, until the sugar has dissolved completely, then boil the syrup for 3–5 minutes until it is just beginning to turn golden.

7 Quickly pour the nut mixture on to the oiled baking sheet and leave it to cool and harden.

8 Stir the cream into the custard and churn in an ice cream maker until stiff but too soft to scoop. Scrape into a tub.

9 Smash the nut brittle (praline) with a rolling pin to break off about a third. Reserve this for the decoration.

10 Put the rest of the nut brittle into a strong plastic bag and hit it with a rolling pin until it breaks into bite-size pieces.

11 Fold the crushed nut brittle into the ice cream and freeze it for 2–3 hours until firm.

12 Scoop the ice cream into glasses and decorate with the reserved nut brittle, broken into large pieces.

Cashew and Orange Flower Ice Cream

Delicately perfumed with orange flower water and a little orange rind, this nutty, lightly sweetened ice cream evokes the aromatic milk puddings that are popular in the Middle East.

SERVES FOUR TO SIX

INGREDIENTS

4 EGG YOLKS

75g|3oz|6 tbsp CASTER
(SUPERFINE) SUGAR

5ml|1 tsp CORNFLOUR
(CORNSTARCH)

300ml|½ pint|1¼ cups
SEMI-SKIMMED (LOW-FAT) MILK

300ml|½ pint|1¼ cups
WHIPPING CREAM

150g|5oz|1¼ cups CASHEW NUTS,
finely chopped

15ml|1 tbsp ORANGE
FLOWER WATER

grated rind of ½ ORANGE,
plus CURLS OF THINLY PARED
ORANGE RIND, to decorate

1 Whisk the egg yolks, caster sugar and cornflour in a large bowl until the mixture is thick and foamy.

2 Pour the semi-skimmed milk into a heavy pan, gently bring it to the boil over a low heat, then gradually whisk it into the egg yolk mixture in the bowl.

3 Return to the pan and cook over a gentle heat, stirring constantly until smooth. Pour back into the bowl. Cool, then chill.

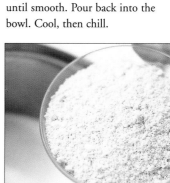

4 Heat the cream in a small pan. When it boils, stir in the chopped cashew nuts. Leave to cool.

5 Stir the orange flower water and grated orange rind into the chilled custard. Process the nut cream in a food processor or blender until it forms a fine paste, then stir it into the custard mixture.

6 Churn the mixture until it is firm enough to scoop.

7 Thinly pare the orange rind, then wrap each strip in turn around a cocktail stick (toothpick) and leave it for a minute or two.

8 To serve, scoop the ice cream into dishes and decorate each portion with an orange rind curl.

Pistachio Ice Cream

SERVES FOUR TO SIX

This universal favourite owes its enduring popularity to its delicate pale green colour and distinctive yet subtle flavour. Buy the pistachio nuts as you need them, as they quickly go stale if left in the cupboard.

INGREDIENTS

4 EGG YOLKS

75g|3oz|6 tbsp CASTER (SUPERFINE) SUGAR

5ml|1 tsp CORNFLOUR (CORNSTARCH)

300ml|½ pint|1¼ cups SEMI-SKIMMED (LOW-FAT) MILK

115g|4oz|1 cup PISTACHIOS, plus a few extra, to decorate

300ml|½ pint|1¼ cups WHIPPING CREAM

a little GREEN FOOD COLOURING

CHOCOLATE-DIPPED WAFFLE CONES, to serve (optional)

1 Place the egg yolks, sugar and cornflour in a bowl and whisk until the mixture is thick and foamy.

2 Pour the milk into a heavy pan, gently bring it to the boil, then gradually whisk it into the egg yolk mixture.

3 Return the mixture to the pan and cook it over a gentle heat, stirring constantly until the custard thickens and is smooth.

4 Pour the custard back into the bowl, set aside to cool, then chill in the refrigerator until required.

5 Shell the pistachios and put them in a food processor or blender. Add 30ml|2 tbsp of the cream and grind the mixture to a coarse paste.

6 Pour the rest of the cream into a small pan. Bring it to the boil, stir in the coarsely ground pistachios, then leave to cool.

7 Mix the chilled custard and pistachio cream together and tint the mixture delicately with a few drops of food colouring.

COOK'S TIP *Bought waffle cones can be decorated by dipping them in melted chocolate and sprinkling them with extra chopped pistachios.*

8 Churn the mixture in an ice cream maker until firm enough to scoop. Serve in cones or dishes, sprinkled with extra pistachios.

modern
favourites

From rich, gooey chocolate brownies to crunchy, tangy strawberry pavlova, this chapter incorporates many family favourites, transforming hot and cold puddings and teatime cakes into delicious ice creams. This modern twist on classic treats will be loved by young and old alike.

White Chocolate and Brownie Ice Cream

This recipe combines an irresistible contrast between creamy white chocolate ice cream and chocolate brownie pieces. Use good quality, bought chocolate brownies, or better still, make your own.

SERVES SIX

INGREDIENTS

4 EGG YOLKS

2.5ml|½ tsp CORNFLOUR
(CORNSTARCH)

300ml|½ pint|1¼ cups
FULL CREAM (WHOLE) MILK

200g|7oz WHITE CHOCOLATE,
CHOPPED

200g|7oz CHOCOLATE BROWNIES

300ml|½ pint|1¼ cups
WHIPPING CREAM

1 Put the egg yolks and cornflour in a bowl and whisk lightly to combine. Bring the milk to the boil in a heavy pan. Pour the milk over the whisked mixture, whisking well to combine.

2 Pour the custard back into the pan and cook over a very gentle heat, stirring continually until slightly thickened.

3 Pour into a bowl and add the chopped chocolate. Leave until the chocolate has melted, stirring frequently. Leave to cool.

4 Crumble the brownies into small pieces. Stir the cream into the chocolate custard and pour into the ice cream maker. Churn the mixture until it is thick.

5 Sprinkle the crumbled brownies over the custard and churn until just mixed. Scoop into glasses or transfer to a freezer container and freeze until ready to serve.

VARIATION *As an alternative, you could use chopped dark (bittersweet) chocolate in place of the white chocolate, and white chocolate brownies or "blondies" in place of the dark chocolate brownies.*

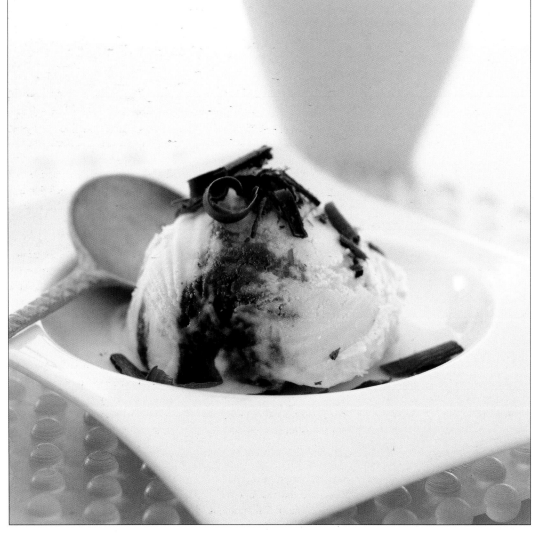

Apple Crumble Ice Cream

*The flavours of this tangy, buttery apple crumble flavoured ice cream are so like the recipe it is based on
that it provides a perfect refreshing alternative to the hot pudding on a summer's day.*

SERVES SIX

INGREDIENTS

4 EGG YOLKS

90g|3½oz|½ cup CASTER
(SUPERFINE) SUGAR

2.5ml|½ tsp CORNFLOUR
(CORNSTARCH)

1.5ml|¼ tsp GROUND CLOVES

300ml|½ pint|1¼ CUPS FULL
CREAM (WHOLE) MILK

65g|2½oz|9 tbsp PLAIN
(ALL-PURPOSE) FLOUR

40g|1½oz|3 tbsp UNSALTED
(SWEET) BUTTER, diced

4 EATING APPLES,
peeled, cored and chopped

300ml|½ pint|1¼ cups
WHIPPING CREAM

1 Whisk the egg yolks, 75g|3oz|
scant ½ cup of the sugar, the
cornflour and ground cloves in a
large bowl. Bring the milk just to
the boil in a heavy pan over a
medium heat.

2 Pour the milk over the whisked
mixture, whisking well to combine.
Pour the custard back into the pan
and cook over a very gentle heat,
stirring until slightly thickened.

3 Tip into a bowl and leave to
cool completely.

4 Preheat the oven to 200°C|400°F|
Gas 6. Lightly grease a baking sheet.
Put the flour in a food processor
with the butter and blend until it
resembles breadcrumbs.

5 Add the remaining sugar and
blend lightly until beginning to bind
together. Tip out on to a baking
sheet and spread in a thin layer.
Bake in the oven for 15–20 minutes
until golden. Leave to cool.

6 Put the apples in a heavy pan
with 60ml|4 tbsp of water. Cover
with a lid and cook very gently for
10 minutes or until the apples have
softened. Tip the cooked apples
into a food processor and blend
until smooth.

7 Stir the whipping cream into
the custard and pour into the
ice cream maker. Churn until it
has a soft set consistency.

8 Reserve 30ml|2 tbsp crumble
mixture and add the remainder to
the ice cream maker. Churn very
lightly until mixed.

9 Spoon one third of the ice cream
into a freezer container and spoon
over half the apple purée. Add half
the remaining ice cream and the
remaining apple purée. Add the rest
of the ice cream.

10 Using a knife, very lightly swirl
the ingredients together so that the
apple is partially mixed into the ice
cream. Freeze for at least 2 hours
or until ready to serve.

Strawberry Pavlova Ice Cream

This ice cream contains all the ingredients of a pavlova dessert and is equally good. For best results serve when strawberries are in season and at their sweetest and most delicious.

SERVES SIX

INGREDIENTS

3 EGG YOLKS plus 2 EGG WHITES

150g|5oz|¾ cup CASTER (SUPERFINE) SUGAR

5ml|1 tsp VANILLA ESSENCE (EXTRACT)

2.5ml|½ tsp CORNFLOUR (CORNSTARCH)

300ml|½ pint|1¼ cups MILK

300g|11oz|2¾ cups STRAWBERRIES

300ml|½ pint|1¼ cups DOUBLE (HEAVY) CREAM

STRAWBERRIES, to decorate

VARIATION *You could make this crunchy ice cream using any puréed summer fruits, such as raspberries, redcurrants and blackcurrants or even peaches or nectarines.*

1 Preheat the oven to 140°C| 275°F|Gas 1. Line a baking sheet with baking parchment. Whisk the egg whites thoroughly in a clean bowl until stiff.

2 Gradually whisk in 90g|3½oz| ½ cup of the sugar, a little at a time, whisking well after each addition until the meringue is stiff and glossy. Whisk in the vanilla with the last of the sugar.

3 Place 8–10 spoonfuls of the mixture on the baking sheet. Bake for about 1 hour or until crispy on the outside. Leave to cool.

4 Mix the remaining sugar in a bowl with the egg yolks and cornflour. Bring the milk just to the boil in a heavy pan. Pour the milk over the whisked mixture, whisking well to combine.

5 Pour the custard back into the pan and cook over a very gentle heat, stirring until slightly thickened. Pour into a bowl and leave to cool completely.

6 Purée the strawberries in a food processor or blender until smooth.

7 Roughly break the meringues into small pieces using your hands. Stir the cream into the custard and pour the mixture into the ice cream maker. Churn until it has a softly set consistency.

8 Scatter a layer of the broken meringues into a freezer container and spoon over a little of the ice cream mixture, spreading it to the edges. Spoon over a little of the strawberry purée.

9 Repeat the layering until all the ingredients are used then press the surface down lightly to level it. Freeze for at least 2 hours or until ready to serve.

10 Scoop the ice cream into glasses and serve decorated with the extra strawberries.

Raspberry Cheesecake Ice Cream

This is a very quick and easy ice cream that looks stunning and tastes gorgeous.

SERVES SIX

INGREDIENTS

300g|11oz|2 cups RASPBERRIES,
plus extra to decorate

90g|3½oz|scant 1 cup ICING
(CONFECTIONER'S) SUGAR,
plus 15ml|1tbsp

200g|7oz|scant 1 cup
CREAM CHEESE

250g|9oz|generous 1 cup
MASCARPONE

5ml|1 tsp VANILLA ESSENCE
(EXTRACT)

300ml|½ pint|1¼ cups DOUBLE
(HEAVY) CREAM

150ml|¼ pint|⅔ cup FULL CREAM
(WHOLE) MILK

1 Thoroughly blend the raspberries in a food processor or blender until they form a smooth purée. Press the purée through a sieve (strainer) set over a bowl (to remove any seeds) and stir in 15ml|1 tbsp of the icing sugar. Chill the raspberry purée until it is needed.

2 Beat the cream cheese in a bowl to soften, then beat in the mascarpone, vanilla, cream, milk and remaining icing sugar until smooth. Stir in 60ml|4 tbsp of the fruit purée. Scrape into the ice cream maker and churn until thick.

3 Transfer one third of the ice cream into a freezer container, spreading it in a thin layer, and spoon over half of the remaining raspberry purée. Top with half of the remaining ice cream and the remaining purée, then add the rest of the ice cream.

4 Using a knife, stir through the ice cream two or three times to ripple the flavours together. Freeze for at least 2 hours until set.

5 Serve scooped into glasses, decorated with fresh raspberries.

VARIATION *As an alternative, use really full-flavoured strawberries instead of raspberries to ripple the cheesecake cream.*

Lemon Meringue Ice Cream

This ice cream contains the delicious combination of tangy lemon and sweet, crunchy pieces of meringue.

SERVES SIX

INGREDIENTS

4 EGG YOLKS, plus 2 EGG WHITES

150g|5oz|¾ cup CASTER (SUPERFINE) SUGAR

finely grated rind of 2 LEMONS, plus 60ml|4 tbsp JUICE

2.5ml|½ tsp CORNFLOUR (CORNSTARCH)

300ml|½ pint|1¼ cups MILK

130g|4½oz LEMON CURD

300ml|½ pint|1¼ cups WHIPPING CREAM

1 Preheat the oven to 140°C| 275°F|Gas 1. Line a baking sheet with baking parchment.

2 Whisk the egg whites in a clean bowl until stiff. Gradually whisk in 90g|3½oz|½ cup of the sugar, a little at a time, whisking well after each addition until the meringue is stiff and glossy. Whisk in the lemon rind with the last of the sugar.

3 Place small spoonfuls of the meringue on the baking sheet.

4 Bake in the oven for about 1–1½ hours or until the meringues are crisp. Leave to cool.

5 Mix the remaining sugar in a bowl with the egg yolks and the cornflour. Bring the milk just to the boil in a heavy pan. Pour the milk over the whisked egg yolk and sugar mixture, whisking well to combine.

6 Pour the custard back into the pan and cook over a very gentle heat, stirring continuously until it is slightly thickened. Turn the mixture into a bowl and leave to cool completely.

7 Lightly crush the cooled meringues. Tip the lemon curd into a bowl and stir in the lemon juice. Add the cream to the custard and pour into the ice cream maker. Churn until the ice cream has a soft set consistency.

8 Spoon a third of the ice cream into a freezer container and scatter with a third of the crushed meringues. Spoon over one third of the lemon sauce. Repeat the layering process, finishing with a layer of sauce.

9 Lightly swirl the mixture together and level the surface. Freeze for at least 2 hours before serving in scoops.

Black Forest Gâteau Ice Cream

All the flavours of boozy soaked dark cherries, cream and chocolate sponge combined in a light ice cream dessert – wicked!

SERVES SIX

INGREDIENTS

425g|15oz can BLACK CHERRIES

90ml|6 tbsp KIRSCH

4 EGG YOLKS

75g|3oz|6 tbsp CASTER
(SUPERFINE) SUGAR

5ml|1 tsp CORNFLOUR
(CORNSTARCH)

300ml|½ pint|1¼ cups SEMI-
SKIMMED (LOW-FAT) MILK

300ml|½ pint|1¼ cups DOUBLE
(HEAVY) CREAM

6 DOUBLE CHOCOLATE
MUFFINS, each one weighing about
75g|3oz

To decorate

FRESH CHERRIES, on stalks

a little sifted COCOA POWDER
(UNSWEETENED)

1 Drain the cherries, discarding the juice then put into a bowl and spoon over 30ml|2 tbsp of the Kirsch. Leave to soak for 2 hours or overnight.

2 Whisk the egg yolks, sugar and cornflour together in a bowl until thick and pale. Pour the milk into a heavy pan, bring it just to the boil, then gradually pour it on to the egg yolk mixture, whisking constantly.

3 Return the mixture to the pan and cook over a gentle heat, stirring constantly until the custard thickens and is smooth. Pour it back into the bowl, cover, leave to cool, then chill well.

4 Stir the cream into the custard then pour into an ice cream maker. Churn until thick.

5 Gradually mix in the soaked cherries and any Kirsch juices and gently churn together.

6 Meanwhile, cut each muffin into three horizontal slices and drizzle with the remaining Kirsch.

7 To serve, sandwich the muffin slices back together with ice cream, arrange on serving plates and decorate with the fresh cherries and a light dusting of cocoa powder.

COOK'S TIP *The juices from the cherries could be made into a sauce by flavouring with a little extra Kirsch and thickening with a little cornflour (cornstarch).*

Minty Madness Ice Cream

This creamy smooth peppermint ice cream is speckled with crushed peppermints and shards of
chocolate-covered peppermint crisps, for a really refreshing flavour.

SERVES SIX

INGREDIENTS

4 EGG YOLKS

75g|3oz|6 tbsp CASTER
(SUPERFINE) SUGAR

5ml|1 tsp CORNFLOUR
(CORNSTARCH)

300ml|½ pint|1¼ cups
SEMI-SKIMMED
(LOW-FAT) MILK

250ml|8fl oz|1 cup
CRÈME FRAÎCHE

5ml|1 tsp PEPPERMINT ESSENCE
(EXTRACT)

50g|2oz MINT IMPERIALS or
OTHER HARD MINTS

75g|3oz CHOCOLATE-COVERED
PEPPERMINT CRISPS

CHOCOLATE CASES, to serve
(optional; see Cook's Tip)

1 Whisk the egg yolks, sugar and cornflour together in a bowl until thick and pale. Pour the milk into a heavy pan, bring it just to the boil, then gradually pour it on to the yolk mixture, whisking constantly.

2 Return the mixture to the pan and cook over a gentle heat, stirring constantly until the custard thickens and is smooth. Pour it back into the bowl, cover, cool then chill.

3 Whisk the crème fraîche and peppermint essence into the chilled custard.

4 Pour into an ice cream maker and churn until thick.

VARIATION *If you can't find or do not like mint Imperials you could substitute either more chocolate-covered peppermint crisps or some plain chocolate chips for the mint candies.*

5 Put the mint Imperials into a plastic bag and beat them with a rolling pin until roughly crushed. Roughly chop the chocolate-covered sweets with a knife.

6 Stir both into the ice cream and churn until firm enough to scoop. Transfer to a freezer container and freeze until required.

7 Scoop into glasses or chocolate cases and sprinkle with extra pieces of chocolate-covered peppermint crisps.

COOK'S TIP *To make the chocolate cases: Spread 175g\6oz melted chocolate over 6 squares of baking parchment to make swirly edged circles about 13cm\5in in diameter. Drape over upturned tumblers so that the chocolate is on the outside.*
Leave to cool and harden, transferring to the refrigerator if necessary. Ease off the tumblers then gently peel away the paper from inside the cups.

Ginger Crunch Ice Cream

This ice cream features smooth mascarpone mixed with vanilla custard and flavoured with hot peppery stem ginger and crunchy pieces of ginger nut biscuit. Serve on its own or on thin slices of gingerbread.

SERVES SIX

INGREDIENTS

4 EGG YOLKS

75g|3oz|6 tbsp CASTER (SUPERFINE) SUGAR

5ml|1 tsp CORNFLOUR (CORNSTARCH)

300ml|½ pint|1¼ cups SEMI-SKIMMED (LOW-FAT) MILK

250g|9 oz|generous 1 cup MASCARPONE

5ml|1 tsp VANILLA ESSENCE (EXTRACT)

50g|2oz PRESERVED STEM GINGER, drained and finely chopped

75g|3oz GINGER NUT BISCUITS (GINGERSNAPS)

PRESERVED STEM GINGER, sliced, to decorate

1 Whisk the egg yolks, sugar and cornflour together in a bowl until thick and pale. Pour the milk into a heavy pan, bring it just to the boil, then gradually pour it on to the egg yolk mixture, whisking constantly.

2 Return the mixture to the pan and cook over a gentle heat, stirring constantly until the custard thickens and is smooth.

3 Pour the mixture back into the bowl, add the mascarpone and vanilla essence and whisk until the cheese has melted. Cover, leave to cool, then chill.

4 Mix the chopped ginger into the mascarpone custard then pour into an ice cream maker. Churn until softly spoonable.

5 Put the biscuits in a strong plastic bag and break into small pieces with a rolling pin, or snap into pieces by hand.

6 Spoon the ice cream into a freezer container, mix in the broken biscuits, cover and transfer to the freezer for 2 hours or until firm enough to scoop.

7 Scoop the ice cream into dishes and decorate with a little extra sliced stem ginger.

COOK'S TIP *It is best to eat this ice cream soon after you have made it or else the biscuits may lose some of their crunch.*

Rainbow Ice Cream

Speckled with roughly chopped sugar-coated sweets this will soon be a family favourite with youngsters and adults alike, and it is especially good at children's parties.

SERVES SIX

INGREDIENTS

4 EGG YOLKS

75g|3oz|6 tbsp CASTER (SUPERFINE) SUGAR

5ml|1 tsp CORNFLOUR (CORNSTARCH)

300ml|½ pint|1¼ cups SEMI-SKIMMED (LOW-FAT) MILK

300ml|½ pint|1¼ cups DOUBLE (HEAVY) CREAM

5ml|1 tsp VANILLA ESSENCE (EXTRACT)

115g|4oz SUGAR-COATED CHOCOLATE SWEETS (M&M's or Smarties)

WHOLE SWEETS (CANDIES), to decorate

1 Whisk the egg yolks, sugar and cornflour together in a bowl until thick and pale. Pour the milk into a heavy pan, bring it just to the boil, then gradually pour it on to the egg yolk mixture in the bowl, whisking constantly.

COOK'S TIP *The sugar coating on the sweets will dissolve into the ice cream, but this just adds to the swirly coloured effect.*

2 Return the mixture to the pan and cook over a gentle heat, stirring constantly until the custard thickens and is smooth.

3 Pour it back into the bowl, cover, leave to cool, then chill.

4 Mix the cream and vanilla essence into the cooled custard, then pour into an ice cream maker. Churn until thick.

5 Roughly chop the sweets, stir them into the ice cream and churn for a minute or two until firm enough to scoop. Transfer to a plastic container and freeze until it is required.

6 Scoop into bowls or cones and decorate with a few whole sweets.

Christmas Pudding Ice Cream

This ice cream is lighter than a traditional Christmas pudding, but with all the festive flavours.

SERVES SIX

INGREDIENTS

75g|3oz|½ cup MIXED DRIED FRUIT

50g|2oz|¼ cup DRIED APRICOTS, diced

50g|2oz|¼ CUP GLACÉ (CANDIED) CHERRIES, quartered

1.5ml|¼ tsp GROUND CINNAMON

grated rind and juice of 1 ORANGE

30ml|2 tbsp SWEET SHERRY or BRANDY

4 EGG YOLKS

75g|3oz|scant 1 cup CASTER (SUPERFINE) SUGAR

5ml|1 tsp CORNFLOUR (CORNSTARCH)

300ml|½ pint|1¼ cups SEMI-SKIMMED (LOW-FAT) MILK

250ml|8fl oz|1 cup CRÈME FRAÎCHE

5ml|1 tsp VANILLA ESSENCE (EXTRACT)

50g|2oz|½ cup PISTACHIO NUTS, HAZELNUTS or PECAN NUTS, or a mixture, roughly chopped

CHOCOLATE HOLLY or SUGAR-COATED BAY LEAVES, to decorate (see Cook's Tip)

THIN SHORTBREAD BISCUITS, to serve

1 Put the dried fruits, cherries, cinnamon, orange rind and juice and sherry or brandy in a small pan and bring the liquid just to the boil. Turn off the heat and leave the mixture to cool for 2 hours or overnight to allow the fruit to plump up.

2 Whisk the egg yolks, sugar and cornflour together in a bowl until the mixture is thick and pale. Heat the milk in a pan then gradually whisk into the yolk mixture. Return the mixture to the pan and cook over a gentle heat, stirring constantly.

COOK'S TIP *To make chocolate holly leaves, paint melted dark (bittersweet) chocolate over washed and dried holly leaves. Set aside to chill and set and then peel away the leaf to reveal the chocolate copy. Alternatively, to make sugar-coated bay leaves, paint washed and dried leaves with egg white, then dip in caster (superfine) sugar and leave to dry.*

3 When the custard thickens and is smooth, pour it back into the bowl. Cover, cool then chill.

4 Whisk the crème fraîche and vanilla essence into the chilled custard, pour into an ice cream maker and churn until thick.

5 Add the fruits and nuts and churn together briefly until just mixed. Spoon into a freezer container, cover and freeze for 2 hours or until firm enough to scoop.

6 Scoop into glasses, decorate with chocolate holly leaves or sugar-coated bay leaves and serve with thin shortbread biscuits.

herb, spice & flower ices

For those with an adventurous taste in ice cream, here is an intriguing repertoire of less predictable flavours such as Turkish delight, lavender and even chilli. The ices in the following collection are quick and easy to make, and will have everyone guessing the elusive ingredients.

Rosemary Ice Cream

Fresh rosemary has a lovely fragrance that works as well in sweet dishes as it does in savoury.

Serve this ice cream as an accompaniment to soft fruit or plum compote, or on its own,

with amaretti or ratafia biscuits.

SERVES SIX

INGREDIENTS

300ml|½ pint|1¼ cups MILK

4 large FRESH
ROSEMARY SPRIGS

3 EGG YOLKS

75g|3oz|6 tbsp CASTER
(SUPERFINE) SUGAR

10ml|2 tsp CORNFLOUR
(CORNSTARCH)

400ml|14fl oz|1⅔ cups
CRÈME FRAÎCHE

about 15ml|1 tbsp DEMERARA
(RAW) SUGAR

FRESH ROSEMARY SPRIGS
and HERB FLOWERS,
to decorate

RATAFIA BISCUITS (COOKIES),
to serve

1 Put the milk and rosemary sprigs in a heavy pan. Bring almost to the boil, remove from the heat and leave to infuse for about 20 minutes. Place the egg yolks in a bowl and whisk in the sugar and the cornflour.

2 Remove the rosemary sprigs. Return the pan to the heat and bring the milk almost to the boil. Gradually pour over the yolk mixture and mix well. Return to the pan and cook over a gentle heat, stirring constantly until it thickens. Do not let it boil.

3 Strain the custard through a sieve (strainer) into a bowl. Cover the surface of the custard closely with baking parchment and leave the mixture to cool. Chill the custard until it is very cold, then stir in the crème fraîche, mixing well to combine thoroughly.

4 Churn the mixture in an ice cream maker until it is thick, then scrape it into a tub or similar freezerproof container. Freeze until ready to serve.

5 Soften the ice cream in the refrigerator for 30 minutes before serving. Scoop into dessert dishes, sprinkle lightly with demerara sugar and decorate with fresh rosemary sprigs and herb flowers. Serve with ratafia biscuits.

COOK'S TIP *For a stylish and attractive effect, use sprigs or petals of herb flowers that complement the colour of your dessert dishes.*

Lavender and Honey Ice Cream

Lavender and honey make a memorable partnership in this old-fashioned and elegant ice cream.

Serve scooped into glasses or set in little moulds and top with lightly whipped cream.

Pretty lavender flowers add the finishing touch.

SERVES SIX TO EIGHT

INGREDIENTS

90ml|6 tbsp CLEAR HONEY

4 EGG YOLKS

10ml|2 tsp CORNFLOUR
(CORNSTARCH)

8 LAVENDER SPRIGS,
plus extra, to decorate

450ml|¾ pint|scant 2 cups MILK

450ml|¾ pint|scant 2 cups
WHIPPING CREAM

DESSERT BISCUITS (COOKIES),
to serve

1 Put the honey, egg yolk, and cornflour in a bowl. Separate the lavender flowers and add them to the bowl, plus a little milk. Whisk lightly. In a heavy pan bring the remaining milk just to the boil. Add the hot milk to the egg yolk mixture, stirring well.

2 Return the mixture to the pan and cook very gently, stirring until the mixture thickens. Pour the custard into a bowl, cover the surface closely with a circle of baking parchment and leave to cool, then chill the mixture until it is very cold.

3 Stir the cream into the custard, then churn the mixture in an ice cream maker until it holds its shape. Transfer to a tub or similar freezerproof container and freeze until ready to serve.

4 Soften the ice cream in the refrigerator for 30 minutes before serving. Scoop into small dishes, decorate with lavender flowers and serve with dessert biscuits.

COOK'S TIP *For a stronger lavender flavour use lavender honey.*

Strawberry and Rose Water Ice Cream

A light, delicate ice cream made with strawberry purée, thick creamy Greek yogurt and just a hint of rose water.

If you can't get fresh strawberries, then thawed frozen ones will work just as well.

SERVES FOUR TO SIX

INGREDIENTS

450g|1lb|4 cups STRAWBERRIES

2 EGG WHITES

75g|3oz|6 tbsp CASTER (SUPERFINE) SUGAR

300ml|½ pint|1¼ cups GREEK (US STRAINED PLAIN) YOGURT

15-20ml| 3–4 tsp ROSE WATER

To decorate

small STRAWBERRIES, halved

ROSE PETALS, washed and dried

tiny, CRISP BISCUITS (COOKIES)

1 Wash and hull the strawberries, then place them in a liquidiser or food processor and purée until smooth. Press the purée through a sieve (strainer) into a bowl and discard the seeds.

2 Whisk the egg whites until they form stiff, moist-looking peaks. Gradually whisk in the sugar one teaspoon at a time and continue whisking for several more minutes until thick and glossy.

3 Fold the strawberry purée into the meringue mixture, then fold in the yogurt. Add enough rose water to taste (see Cook's Tip).

4 Pour into an ice cream maker and churn until thick enough to scoop. Transfer to a freezer container and freeze until required.

5 Spoon into dishes and decorate with halved strawberries. Serve with tiny crisp biscuits.

COOK'S TIP *Rose water varies in strength, so add it little by little and taste the mixture as you go.*

If you happen to have pink roses in the garden, then decorate the scooped ice cream with a few pink petals for an extra special touch.

Peppermint Swirl Ice Cream

Delicately marbled with a pale green tinged syrup, this sophisticated yogurt ice cream is ideal for serving after a rich main course.

SERVES SIX

INGREDIENTS

75g|3oz|6 tbsp CASTER (SUPERFINE) SUGAR

60ml|4 tbsp WATER

10 large FRESH PEPPERMINT SPRIGS

5ml|1 tsp PEPPERMINT ESSENCE (EXTRACT)

450ml|¾ pint|scant 2 cups DOUBLE (HEAVY) CREAM

a few drops of GREEN FOOD COLOURING

200ml|7fl oz|scant 1 cup GREEK (US STRAINED PLAIN) YOGURT

To decorate

FRESH MINT LEAVES

sifted ICING (CONFECTIONERS') SUGAR

1 Put the sugar, water and fresh peppermint sprigs in a small heavy pan and heat gently, stirring occasionally, until the sugar has dissolved. Bring to the boil and cook without stirring for about 3 minutes to make a syrup.

2 Strain the syrup into a medium bowl and stir in the peppermint essence then leave to cool.

3 Mix half the peppermint mixture with 30ml|2 tbsp of the cream and a few drops of food colouring, then chill until required.

4 Mix the remaining mint syrup with the remaining cream and the yogurt. Pour into the ice cream maker and churn until thick.

5 Spoon the mixture into a freezer container in layers, alternating with spoonfuls of the reserved coloured mint cream.

6 Using a dessertspoon handle, gently stir the mixtures together with five or six strokes until it is all marbled together.

7 Freeze the ice cream for 2 hours or until it is firm.

8 Scoop the ice cream into dishes and decorate with mint leaves that have been dusted lightly with sifted icing sugar.

Basil and Orange Sorbet

Basil has a sweet, aromatic flavour that goes very well with citrus fruits. This delicious, fragrant sorbet is refreshing and not too cloying, so it would be perfect after a rich main course or to relax with on a hot summer's afternoon.

SERVES SIX

INGREDIENTS

175g|6oz|scant 1 cup CASTER (SUPERFINE) SUGAR

105ml|7 tbsp WATER

30ml|2 tbsp LEMON or LIME JUICE

500ml|17fl oz|generous 2 cups FRESHLY SQUEEZED ORANGE JUICE

15g|½oz FRESH BASIL LEAVES

TINY BASIL LEAVES, to decorate

1 Put the sugar and water in a pan and bring slowly to the boil, stirring until all of the sugar has dissolved. Leave the liquid to cool and then stir in the lemon or lime juice.

2 Put half the orange juice in a food processor or blender with the basil leaves and process the mixture in short bursts until the basil has been chopped into small pieces.

3 Pour the syrup, basil specked orange juice and remaining orange juice into the ice cream maker and churn until thick.

4 Scoop into bowls and decorate with basil leaves or turn into a freezer container and freeze until it is required.

COOK'S TIP *Buy good quality freshly squeezed orange juice, or alternatively you could squeeze your own. You'll need 10–12 small juicing oranges.*

Star Anise and Grapefruit Water Ice

This mildly spiced, refreshing water ice is softer and slushier than a sorbet.

Once the syrup is made, the whole star anise can be set aside for decoration. If the ones you buy

are broken up, use the equivalent of six whole ones for the syrup infusion.

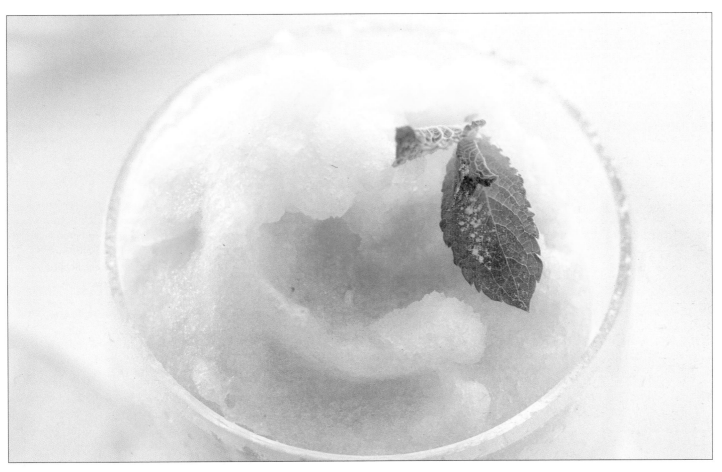

SERVES FOUR

INGREDIENTS

200g|7oz|1 cup CASTER (SUPERFINE) SUGAR

300ml|½ pint|1¼ cups WATER

6 whole STAR ANISE

4 GRAPEFRUITS

1 Put the sugar and water in a pan and heat gently, stirring occasionally, until the sugar has dissolved. Stir in the star anise and heat the syrup gently for 2 minutes. Leave to cool.

VARIATION *This water ice could also be made using blood oranges in place of the grapefruit for a dramatic and refreshing alternative.*

2 Take a slice off the top and base of each grapefruit, then peel off the skin and pith. If you want to use the skin as a bowl, slice the fruit in half and carefully cut out the flesh, leaving the pith behind.

3 Chop the flesh of the grapefruit roughly and put it in a food processor with any juice.

4 Process the grapefruit flesh until it is almost smooth, then press the pulp through a sieve (strainer) into a bowl. Discard any pith that is left behind in the sieve.

5 Strain the star anise and sugar syrup through the sieve into the bowl containing the strained grapefruit juice.

6 Pour into the ice cream maker and churn until the mixture is thick and slushy.

7 Spoon the water ice into serving bowls or hollowed-out grapefuit shells. If you do not want to eat it immediately, transfer to a freezer container and freeze until ready to serve.

Lemon and Cardamom Ice Cream

The classic partnership of lemon and cardamom gives this rich ice cream a lovely "clean" tang. It is the perfect choice after a spicy main course.

SERVES SIX

INGREDIENTS

15ml|1 tbsp CARDAMOM PODS

4 EGG YOLKS

115g|4oz CASTER (SUPERFINE) SUGAR

10ml|2 tsp CORNFLOUR (CORNSTARCH)

grated rind and juice of 3 LEMONS

300ml|½ pint|1¼ cups MILK

300ml|½ pint|1¼ cups WHIPPING CREAM

FRESH LEMON BALM SPRIGS sprinkled with ICING (CONFECTIONERS') SUGAR, to decorate

1 Put the cardamom pods in a mortar and crush them with a pestle to release the seeds. Pick out and discard the shells, then grind the seeds to break them up slightly.

2 Put the egg yolks, sugar, cornflour, lemon rind and juice in a bowl. Add the cardamom seeds and whisk well.

3 Bring the milk to the boil in a heavy pan, then pour it over the egg yolk mixture, stirring well. Return the mixture to the pan and cook gently, stirring until the custard thickens.

4 Pour the custard into a bowl, cover the surface closely with a circle of baking parchment and leave to cool. Chill until very cold.

5 Whisk the cream lightly into the custard and churn the mixture in an ice cream maker until it holds its shape. Transfer to a container and freeze until needed.

6 Soften the ice cream in the refrigerator for 30 minutes before serving. Scoop into glasses and decorate with the sugar-sprinkled lemon balm sprigs.

COOK'S TIP *Lemon balm is an easy herb to grow. The leaves are best picked before the flowering period, when they are at their most fragrant.*

Saffron, Apricot and Almond Cream

SERVES SIX TO EIGHT

This vibrant, chunky ice cream has a slightly Middle Eastern flavour. Although saffron is expensive, its intense colour and distinctive flavour are well worth it, and you only need a small amount.

INGREDIENTS

150g|5oz|⅔ cup DRIED APRICOTS

60ml|4 tbsp COINTREAU

2.5ml|½ tsp SAFFRON STRANDS, lightly crushed

15ml|1 tbsp BOILING WATER

3 EGG YOLKS

75g|3oz|6 tbsp CASTER (SUPERFINE) SUGAR

10ml|2 tsp CORNFLOUR (CORNSTARCH)

300ml|½ pint|1¼ cups MILK

300ml|½ pint|1¼ cups SINGLE (LIGHT) CREAM

75g|3oz|¾ cup UNBLANCHED ALMONDS, lightly toasted

AMARETTI, to serve (optional)

1 Chop the apricots into small pieces and put them in a bowl. Add the liqueur and leave for about 1 hour or until absorbed. Put the saffron in a cup with the boiling water and leave to stand while you make the custard.

2 Whisk the egg yolks, sugar and cornflour with a little of the milk in a bowl. Pour the remaining milk into a pan, bring it almost to the boil, then pour it over the yolk mixture, stirring.

3 Return the mixture to the pan and cook it over a very gentle heat, stirring until the custard thickens. Do not let it boil or it may curdle.

4 Stir in the saffron, with its liquid, then cover the surface of the custard with baking parchment and leave it to cool. Chill until it is very cold.

5 Stir in the cream and churn in an ice cream maker until thick. Add the apricots and nuts and churn for 5 minutes more until well mixed. Spoon into a plastic tub or similar freezerproof container and freeze overnight.

6 Soften the ice cream in the refrigerator 30 minutes before serving. Scoop into glasses and serve with amaretti.

COOK'S TIP *This ice cream looks most attractive served in small glasses or little glass cups with handles.*

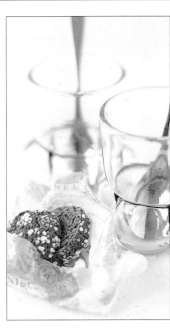

Ginger and Kiwi Sorbet

This refreshing sorbet combines freshly grated aromatic root ginger with sweet kiwi fruit.

SERVES SIX

INGREDIENTS

150g|2oz FRESH ROOT GINGER

115g|4oz|½ cup CASTER (SUPERFINE) SUGAR

300ml|½ pint|1¼ cups WATER

5 KIWI FRUIT

FRESH MINT SPRIGS or CHOPPED KIWI FRUIT, to decorate

1 Peel the ginger and grate it finely. Heat the sugar and water in a pan until the sugar has dissolved. Add the ginger and cook for 1 minute, then leave to cool. Strain into a bowl and chill until very cold.

2 Peel the kiwi fruit and blend until smooth. Add the purée to the chilled syrup and mix well.

3 Churn the mixture in an ice cream maker until it thickens. Transfer to a plastic tub or a similar freezerproof container and freeze until you are ready to serve the sorbet.

4 Spoon into dishes or glasses, decorate with mint sprigs or chopped kiwi fruit, and serve.

Chilli Sorbet

Served during or after dinner this unusual but refreshing sorbet is sure to become a talking point.

SERVES SIX

INGREDIENTS

1 FRESH RED CHILLI

finely grated rind and juice of 2 LEMONS

finely grated rind and juice of 2 LIMES

225g|8oz|1 cup CASTER (SUPERFINE) SUGAR

750ml|1¼ pints|3 cups WATER

PARED LEMON or LIME RIND, to decorate

1 Cut the chilli in half, removing all the seeds and any pith with a small sharp knife, and then chop the flesh very finely.

2 Put the chilli, lemon and lime rind, sugar and water in a heavy pan. Heat gently and stir while the sugar dissolves. Bring to the boil, then simmer for 2 minutes without stirring. Let cool.

3 Add lemon and lime juice to the chilli syrup and chill until very cold.

4 Churn the mixture in an ice cream maker until it holds its shape. Scrape into a container and freeze until ready to serve. Spoon into glasses and decorate with the thinly pared lemon or lime rind.

COOK'S TIP *Use a medium-hot chilli rather than any of the fiery varieties. For an added kick, drizzle with tequila or vodka before serving. To avoid burning your skin, wash your hands after handling the chilli.*

Turkish Delight Sorbet

Anyone who likes Turkish delight will adore the taste and aroma of this intriguing dessert. Because of its sweetness, it is best served in small portions and is delicious with after-dinner coffee. Decorate with drizzled white chocolate and sugared almonds or slices of Turkish delight.

SERVES EIGHT

INGREDIENTS

250g|9oz ROSE WATER-FLAVOURED TURKISH DELIGHT

25g|1oz|2 tbsp CASTER (SUPERFINE) SUGAR

750ml|1¼ pints|3 cups WATER

30ml|2 tbsp LEMON JUICE

50g|2oz WHITE CHOCOLATE, broken into pieces

roughly chopped SUGARED ALMONDS, to decorate

1 Cut the cubes of Turkish delight into small pieces. Put half of the pieces in a heavy pan with the sugar. Pour in half of the water. Heat gently until the Turkish delight has dissolved.

2 Cool, then stir in the lemon juice with the remaining water and Turkish delight. Chill well.

3 Churn the mixture in an ice cream maker until it is firm enough to hold its shape.

COOK'S TIP *You will probably find it easiest to use scissors to cut the cubes of Turkish delight into smaller pieces, rather than a knife.*

If you want to serve the ice cream with Turkish delight instead of sugared almonds, thinly slice 50g|2oz and sprinkle over the top of the ice cream.

4 While the sorbet is freezing, dampen eight very small plastic cups or glasses. Line them with clear film (plastic wrap).

5 Spoon the sorbet into the cups and tap them lightly on the surface to compact the mixture. Cover with the overlapping film and freeze for at least 3 hours or overnight.

6 Make a paper piping (pastry) bag. Put the chocolate in a heatproof bowl and melt it over a pan of gently simmering water.

7 Meanwhile, remove the sorbets from the freezer, let them stand at room temperature for 5 minutes, then pull them out of the cups. Transfer to serving plates and peel away the film. Spoon the melted chocolate into the piping bag, snip off the tip and scribble a design on the sorbet and the plate. Scatter the sugared almonds over and serve.

Mulled Wine Sorbet

This dramatic-looking sorbet provides a brief and welcome respite from the general overindulgence that takes place during the festive season, or any other celebration. It is spicy and flavoursome, with quite a powerful kick to revive you from any seasonal sluggishness!

SERVES SIX

INGREDIENTS

1 bottle MEDIUM RED WINE

2 CLEMENTINES or
1 LARGE ORANGE

16 WHOLE CLOVES

2 CINNAMON STICKS, HALVED

1 APPLE, roughly chopped

5ml|1 tsp MIXED
(APPLE PIE) SPICE

75g|3oz|scant ½ cup LIGHT
MUSCOVADO (BROWN) SUGAR

150ml|¼ pint|⅔ cup WATER

200ml|7fl oz|scant 1 cup
FRESHLY SQUEEZED
ORANGE JUICE

45ml|3 tbsp BRANDY

strips of pared ORANGE RIND,
to decorate

1 Pour the bottle of wine into a pan. Stud the clementines or orange with the cloves, then cut them in half.

2 Add to the wine, with the cinnamon sticks, apple, mixed spice, sugar and water. Heat gently, stirring occasionally, until the sugar has dissolved.

3 Cover the pan and cook the mixture gently for 15 minutes. Remove from the heat and leave it to cool.

4 Pour the mixture through a sieve (strainer) into a large bowl, then stir in the orange juice and brandy. Chill until it is very cold.

5 Churn the mixture in an ice cream maker until it thickens. Transfer to a plastic tub or a similar freezerproof container and freeze until ready to serve.

6 To serve, spoon or scoop into small glasses and decorate with the strips of pared orange rind.

COOK'S TIP *The better the quality of the red wine you use, the better this sorbet will taste, so try to use one of a reasonable standard.*

Elderflower and Lime Yogurt Ice Cream

These fragrant flowerheads have a wonderful flavour, but they are only in season for a very short time. Fortunately, good quality elderflower cordial is readily available and combines beautifully with limes to make a very refreshing iced dessert.

SERVES SIX

INGREDIENTS

4 EGG YOLKS

50g|2oz|¼ cup CASTER (SUPERFINE) SUGAR

10ml|2 tsp CORNFLOUR (CORNSTARCH)

300ml|½ pint|1¼ cups MILK

finely grated rind and juice of 2 LIMES

150ml|¼ pint|⅔ cup ELDERFLOWER CORDIAL

200ml|7fl oz|scant 1 cup GREEK (US STRAINED PLAIN) YOGURT

150ml|¼ pint|⅔ cup DOUBLE (HEAVY) CREAM

GRATED LIME RIND, to decorate

5 Soften the yogurt ice in the refrigerator 30 minutes before serving. Decorate with the grated lime rind.

COOK'S TIP *Yogurt gives this ice cream a slightly tangier flavour than cream, but you can use cream if you prefer.*

3 Pour the custard into a bowl and add the lime rind and juice. Pour in the elderflower cordial and mix lightly. Cover the surface of the mixture closely with baking parchment. Leave to cool, then chill until very cold.

4 Stir the yogurt and cream into the chilled mixture and churn in an ice cream maker until it thickens. Transfer the yogurt ice into individual dishes or a plastic container, cover closely and freeze until required.

1 Whisk the egg yolks in a bowl with the sugar, cornflour and a little of the milk until it is pale and frothy. Pour the remaining milk into a heavy pan, bring it just to the boil, then pour it over the yolk mixture, whisking constantly until it is smooth.

2 Return the mixture to the pan and cook over a very gentle heat, stirring constantly until the custard thickens. Do not let it boil or the mixture may curdle.

Pomegranate and Orange Flower Ice Cream

Take advantage of the availability of fresh pomegranates when in season to make this wonderfully coloured dessert. The colour will range from pastel pink to vibrant cerise, depending on the type of pomegranates used, but whatever shade you achieve the result will be very impressive.

SERVES SIX

INGREDIENTS

10ml|2 tsp CORNFLOUR (CORNSTARCH)

300ml|½ pint|1¼ cups MILK

25g|1oz|2 tbsp CASTER (SUPERFINE) SUGAR

2 LARGE POMEGRANATES

30ml|2 tbsp ORANGE FLOWER WATER

75ml|5 tbsp GRENADINE

300ml|½ pint|1¼ cups WHIPPING CREAM

extra POMEGRANATE SEEDS and ORANGE FLOWER WATER, to serve

1 Put the cornflour in a pan and blend to a paste with a little of the milk. Stir in the remaining milk and the sugar and cook, stirring constantly, until the mixture thickens. Pour it into a bowl, cover the surface closely with baking parchment and leave it to cool.

2 Cut the pomegranates in half and squeeze out the juice, using a lemon squeezer. Add the juice to the cornflour mixture, with the orange flower water, grenadine and cream. Stir lightly to mix.

3 Churn the mixture in an ice cream maker until it is thoroughly combined and thick enough to hold its shape.

4 Spoon the ice cream into one large, or six individual freezerproof serving dishes and freeze for at least 2 hours, or overnight.

5 Soften the frozen ice cream in the refrigerator for 30 minutes before serving, to allow them to soften. Top each serving with pomegranate seeds tossed in the extra orange flower water.

VARIATION *To accentuate the Middle Eastern flavour of this dessert, the seeds from 12 cardamom pods can be added with the orange flower water.*

cream-free, low-fat & low-sugar ices

Whether for health reasons or simply through choice, many people prefer to eat low-fat, low-sugar and dairy-free foods. On the following pages are some intensely flavoured desserts to suit everyone, ranging from a smooth creamy coconut ice to a refreshing orange and yogurt ice.

Kulfi

This famous Indian ice cream is low in sugar and is lightly flavoured with crushed cardamom and finely chopped pistachios. It is traditionally made by slowly boiling milk until it has reduced to almost one-third of its original quantity.

SERVES FOUR

INGREDIENTS

1.5 litres|2½ pints|6¼ cups
FULL-FAT (WHOLE) MILK

3 CARDAMOM PODS

50g|2 oz|¼ cup CASTER
(SUPERFINE) SUGAR

50g|2oz|½ cup PISTACHIO NUTS,
SKINNED, FINELY CHOPPED

To decorate

PINK ROSE PETALS, washed
and dried

thinly sliced PISTACHIO NUTS

1 Pour the milk into a large, heavy pan. Bring to the boil, lower the heat and simmer gently for 1 hour, stirring occasionally. Keep a close eye on the pan to prevent the milk from boiling over.

2 Put the cardamom pods in a mortar and crush them with a pestle. Add the pods and the seeds to the milk and continue simmering for 1–1½ hours until the milk has reduced to 600ml| 1 pint|2½ cups.

3 Pour the milk through a sieve (strainer) into a jug (pitcher), then stir in the sugar and leave the mixture to cool.

4 Pour into an ice cream maker and churn until thick. Mix in the pistachios and churn briefly to combine thoroughly.

5 Scoop the soft ice cream into kulfi moulds. Freeze until firm, or overnight. Alternatively, you could leave the mixture churning in the ice cream machine until it is firm and then simply scoop into shallow bowls straight from the machine.

6 To unmould the kulfi, half fill a plastic container or bowl with very hot water, stand the moulds in the water and count to ten. Lift out the moulds and invert them on a baking sheet.

7 Transfer the ice creams to a platter or individual plates. Scatter with rose petals and the thinly sliced pistachios.

Dondurma Kaymalki

This sweet, pure white ice cream comes from the Middle East, where it is traditionally thickened with sahlab and flavoured with orange flower water and mastic, a resin used in chewing gum. As sahlab and mastic are both difficult to obtain in the West, cornflour and light condensed milk have been used in their place.

SERVES FOUR TO SIX

INGREDIENTS

45ml|3 tbsp CORNFLOUR (CORNSTARCH)

600ml|1 pint|2½ cups SEMI-SKIMMED (LOW-FAT) MILK

213g|7½oz can LIGHT CONDENSED MILK

15ml|1 tbsp CLEAR HONEY

10ml|2 tsp ORANGE FLOWER WATER

a few SUGARED ALMONDS, to serve

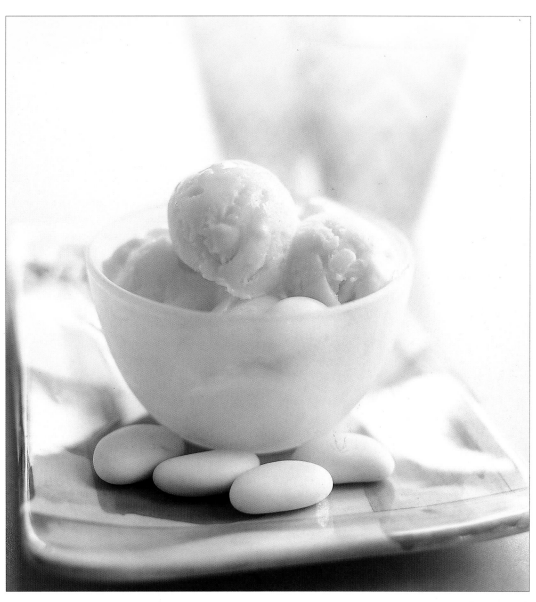

1 Put the cornflour in a pan and mix to a smooth paste with a little of the milk.

2 Stir in the remaining milk and the condensed milk and bring the mixture to the boil, stirring until it has thickened and is smooth. Pour the mixture into a bowl.

3 Stir in the honey and orange flower water. Cover with a plate to prevent the formation of a skin, leave to cool, then chill in the refrigerator until the mixture is completely cold.

4 Churn in an ice cream maker until firm enough to scoop.

5 To serve, scoop into dishes and serve with a few sugared almonds, if liked.

VARIATION *Light condensed milk is surprisingly low in fat, but if you want to make a richer, creamier version, use ordinary sweetened condensed milk and full cream (whole) milk.*
You could also substitute rose water for the orange flower water.

Coconut Ice

Despite its creamy taste, this ice cream contains neither cream nor egg and is very refreshing.

SERVES FOUR TO SIX

INGREDIENTS

150ml|¼ pint|⅔ cup WATER

115g|4oz|½ cup CASTER (SUPERFINE) SUGAR

2 LIMES

400ml|14fl oz can COCONUT MILK

TOASTED COCONUT SHAVINGS, to decorate (see Cook's Tip)

1 Put the water in a small pan. Tip in the caster sugar and bring to the boil, stirring constantly until the sugar has all dissolved. Remove the pan from the heat and leave the syrup to cool, then chill well.

2 Grate the limes finely, taking care to avoid the bitter pith. Squeeze them and pour the juice and rind into the pan of syrup. Add the coconut milk.

3 Churn the mixture in an ice cream maker until firm enough to scoop. Serve in dishes, decorated with the toasted coconut shavings.

COOK'S TIP *Use the flesh from a coconut to make a pretty decoration. Having rinsed the flesh with cold water, cut off thin slices using a swivel-blade vegetable peeler. Toast the slices under a moderate grill (broiler) until the coconut has curled and the edges are golden. Cool slightly, then sprinkle the shavings over the coconut ice.*

Date and Tofu Ice

SERVES FOUR

Generously spiced with cinnamon, this unusual ice cream is packed with soya protein, contains no added sugar, is low in fat and free from all dairy products.

INGREDIENTS

250g|9oz|1½ cups STONED (PITTED) DATES

600ml|1 pint|2½ cups APPLE JUICE

5ml|1 tsp GROUND CINNAMON

285g|10½oz pack CHILLED TOFU, drained and cubed

150ml|¼ pint|⅔ cup UNSWEETENED SOYA MILK

1 Put the dates in a pan. Pour in 300ml|½ pint|1¼ cups of the apple juice and leave to soak for 2 hours. Simmer for 10 minutes, then leave to cool. Using a slotted spoon, lift out one-quarter of the dates, chop roughly and set aside.

2 Purée the remaining dates in a food processor or blender. Add the cinnamon and process with enough of the remaining apple juice to make a smooth paste.

3 Add the cubes of tofu, a few at a time, processing after each addition. Finally, add the remaining apple juice and the soya milk and mix well to combine.

4 Churn the mixture in an ice cream maker until very thick, but not thick enough to scoop. Scrape into a plastic tub.

VARIATION *You could make this tasty ice cream with any soft dried fruits; dried figs, apricots or peaches would be especially good. Alternatively you could use a combination for a vitamin- and fibre-packed feast.*

5 Stir in most of the chopped dates and freeze for 2–3 hours until firm.

6 Scoop into dessert glasses and decorate with the remaining chopped dates.

COOK'S TIP *As tofu is a non-dairy product it will not blend completely, so don't be concerned if the mixture contains tiny flecks of tofu.*

Banana Gelato

This mild, creamy banana ice cream is made with soya milk, making it good for children who are lactose intolerant or allergic to dairy products.

SERVES FOUR TO SIX

INGREDIENTS

115g|4oz|½ cup CASTER (SUPERFINE) SUGAR

150ml|¼ pint|⅔ cup WATER

1 LEMON

3 RIPE BANANAS

300ml|½ pint|1¼ cups UHT VANILLA-FLAVOURED SOYA DESSERT

1 Put the sugar and water in a pan. Bring to the boil, stirring until the sugar has dissolved. Cool.

COOK'S TIP *This recipe makes 1 litre|1¾ pints|4 cups of frozen gelato, so you may need to churn in two batches if your ice cream maker has a small capacity.*

2 Squeeze the lemon. Put the bananas in a bowl and mash with a fork. Slowly add the lemon juice. Stir in the cooled sugar syrup and the soya dessert.

3 Churn in an ice cream maker until thick, then scrape it into a freezerproof container and freeze for 3–4 hours until firm. Scoop into dishes and serve.

Honeyed Goat's Milk Gelato

Goat's milk is more widely available than it used to be and is more easily tolerated by some individuals than cow's milk. It makes a surprisingly rich iced dessert.

SERVES FOUR

INGREDIENTS

6 EGG YOLKS

50g|2oz|¼ cup CASTER (SUPERFINE) SUGAR

10ml|2 tsp CORNFLOUR (CORNSTARCH)

600ml|1 pint|2½ cups GOAT'S MILK

60ml|4 tbsp CLEAR HONEY

POMEGRANATE SEEDS, to decorate

1 Whisk the egg yolks, sugar and cornflour in a large bowl until pale and thick.

2 Pour the goat's milk into a heavy pan, bring it to the boil, then gradually whisk it into the yolk mixture in the bowl.

3 Return the custard mixture to the pan and cook gently over a low heat, stirring constantly until the custard thickens and is smooth. Pour it back into the clean bowl.

4 Stir the honey into the milk mixture. Leave to cool, then chill.

5 Churn the chilled mixture in an ice cream maker until thick enough to scoop.

6 To serve, scoop into dessert glasses and decorate with a few pomegranate seeds.

COOK'S TIP *Make sure the spoon measures are level or the honey flavour will be too dominant.*

VARIATION *This ice cream is also delicious with a little ginger; stir in 40g|1½oz|¼ cup finely chopped preserved stem ginger when the ice cream is partially frozen.*

Raspberry Sherbet

Traditional sherbets are made in much the same way as sorbets but with added milk. This modern low-fat version is made from raspberry purée blended with sugar syrup and virtually fat-free fromage frais, then flecked with crushed raspberries.

SERVES SIX

INGREDIENTS

175g|6oz|¾ cup CASTER (SUPERFINE) SUGAR

150ml|¼ pint|⅔ cup WATER

500g|1¼lb|3½ cups RASPBERRIES, plus extra, to serve

500ml|17fl oz|generous 2 cups VIRTUALLY FAT-FREE FROMAGE FRAIS or CREAM CHEESE

1 Put the sugar and water in a small pan and bring to the boil, stirring until the sugar has dissolved. Pour into a bowl; cool.

2 Put 350g|12oz|2½ cups of the raspberries in a food processor or blender. Process to a purée, then press through a sieve (strainer) placed over a large bowl to remove the seeds. Stir the sugar syrup into the raspberry purée and chill the mixture until it is very cold.

3 Add the fromage frais to the purée and whisk until smooth.

4 Churn the mixture in an ice cream maker until it is thick but too soft to scoop. Scrape into a freezerproof container.

5 Lightly crush the remaining raspberries between your fingers and add them to the partially frozen ice cream. Mix lightly, then freeze for 2–3 hours until firm.

6 Scoop the ice cream into dishes and serve with extra raspberries.

COOK'S TIP *This recipe makes 900ml|1½ pints|3¾ cups of mixture. If this is too large a quantity for your machine, you may need to make it in two batches.*

Orange and Yogurt Ice

Serve this refreshing low-fat yogurt ice simply, in cones, or scoop it into bought or home-made meringue baskets and decorate it with blueberries and mint for a more sophisticated treat. If you want a more decadent dessert, use whipping cream or double (heavy) cream in place of the yogurt.

SERVES SIX

INGREDIENTS

90ml|6 tbsp WATER

10ml|2 tsp POWDERED GELATINE

115g|4oz|½ cup CASTER (SUPERFINE) SUGAR

250ml|8fl oz|1 cup "FRESHLY SQUEEZED" ORANGE JUICE from a carton or bottle

500ml|17fl oz|generous 2 cups NATURAL (PLAIN) YOGURT

CONES or MERINGUE NESTS, BLUEBERRIES and FRESH MINT SPRIGS, to serve

1 Put 30ml|2 tbsp of the water in a small bowl and sprinkle the powdered gelatine over the top. Set aside until spongy.

2 Meanwhile, put the sugar in a small pan, add the remaining water and heat through gently until the sugar has dissolved completely.

3 Take off the heat, add the gelatine and stir until dissolved. Cool, stir in the orange juice and chill for 15–30 minutes.

4 Churn the orange mixture in an ice cream maker until thick, but not thick enough to scoop.

5 Switch off the machine. Remove the paddle, if necessary, add the yogurt to the orange mixture and mix well.

6 Replace the paddle and continue to churn the ice cream for 15–20 minutes until it is thick.

7 Scrape it into a plastic tub or a similar freezerproof container and freeze until firm.

8 Scoop the yogurt ice into cones or meringue nests and decorate with blueberries and mint.

COOK'S TIP *Meringue nests are not difficult to make, but if you do not have the time, bought ones are a perfectly acceptable alternative.*

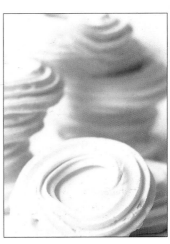

Mango and Lime Ice Cream

This pale golden iced dessert is flavoured with lime syrup and reduced-fat coconut milk for a light fruity finale, perfect to follow an Indian main course.

SERVES SIX

INGREDIENTS

grated rind and juice of 2 LIMES

75g|3oz|scant ½ cup CASTER (SUPERFINE) SUGAR

2 MANGOES, each about 350g|12oz, stoned (pitted) and peeled

400ml|14fl oz|1⅔ cups REDUCED-FAT COCONUT MILK

To decorate

FRESH MANGO slices

LIME RIND curls

1 Put the lime rind and juice into a pan with 45ml|3 tbsp water and the sugar. Heat gently until the sugar has dissolved then bring to the boil.

2 Roughly chop the mango flesh then purée in a liquidizer or food processor until smooth. Mix the purée with the sugar syrup and coconut milk then chill well.

3 Pour the mixture into an ice cream maker and churn until it is firm enough to scoop. Spoon the ice cream into a freezer container and freeze until required.

4 Scoop into glass dishes and decorate with thin slices of mango and curls of lime rind made with a cannelle knife (zester).

VARIATION *A 400g|14oz can of mango pulp could be used instead of fresh mango purée if preferred.*

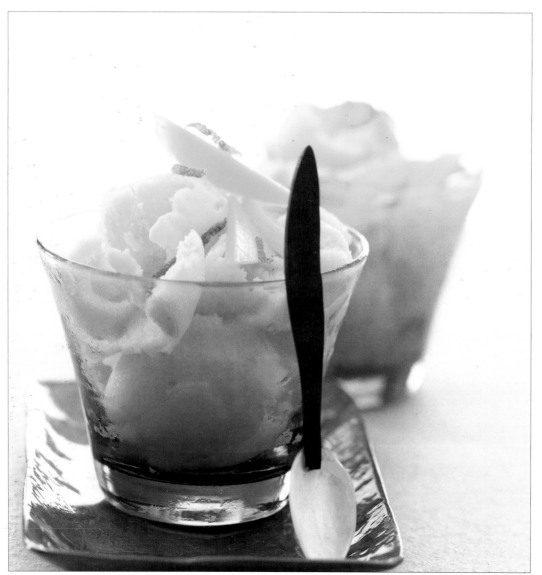

Blueberry and Honey Ripple Ice Cream

Packed with vitamin C, blueberries add a vitamin boost to this light honey-flavoured dessert. Frozen blueberries have been used here as they are a handy standby.

SERVES SIX

INGREDIENTS

4 EGG YOLKS

40g|1½oz|3 tbsp CASTER (SUPERFINE) SUGAR

5ml|1 tsp CORNFLOUR (CORNSTARCH)

300ml|½ pint|1¼ cups SEMI-SKIMMED (LOW-FAT) MILK

60ml|4 tbsp CLEAR HONEY

150g|5oz|1¼ cups FROZEN BLUEBERRIES, defrosted

200g|7oz|scant 1 cup FROMAGE FRAIS OR MASCARPONE

To decorate

BLUEBERRIES

FRESH MINT LEAVES

1 Whisk the yolks, sugar and cornflour together in a bowl until thick and pale. Heat the milk in a pan then gradually whisk into the yolk mixture. Return the mixture to the pan and cook over a gentle heat, stirring all the time.

2 When the custard thickens and is smooth, pour it back into the bowl and stir in the honey. Cover and cool, then chill.

3 Meanwhile, place the blueberries in a liquidizer or food processor until purée until smooth, then press through a sieve (strainer).

4 Mix the fromage frais or mascarpone into the cooled honey custard then pour into an ice cream maker and churn until thick.

5 Take out one third of the ice cream and mix with the blueberry purée. Add alternate spoonfuls of honey ice cream and blueberry ice cream to a freezer container.

6 Using a dessertspoon handle, stir the mixtures together with five or six strokes to give a swirled effect. Cover and freeze until firm enough to scoop.

7 Scoop into glasses and decorate with a few extra blueberries and some mint leaves.

Bloody Mary Sorbet

Invigorating, refreshing and with a mild alcoholic kick, this delicious blend is great at any time,

particularly on a hot summer's day before lunch or supper.

SERVES FOUR

INGREDIENTS

750g|1lb 10oz PASSATA (BOTTLED STRAINED TOMATOES)

2 CELERY STICKS, roughly chopped

30ml|2 tbsp WORCESTERSHIRE SAUCE or 15ml|1 tbsp TABASCO SAUCE

10ml|2 tsp LEMON JUICE

75ml|5 tbsp VODKA

CELERY STICKS, to decorate

1 Put half of the passata in a food processor or blender with the celery, and process until smooth. Press the mixture through a sieve (strainer) into a bowl and stir in the remaining passata.

2 Stir in the Worcestershire or Tabasco sauce, lemon juice and vodka.

3 Pour the mixture into the ice cream maker and churn until thick. Spoon into small glasses and decorate with celery sticks, or transfer to a freezer container and freeze until ready to serve.

COOK'S TIP *Don't be tempted to increase the amount of vodka in the sorbet or it won't freeze. You can always drizzle a little more into the glasses for an extra kick.*

Quantities of this delicious sorbet can easily be increased for a large party, in which case it will need to be churned in batches.

Cinnamon Ricotta Ice with Toasted Granola

Mixed with light, creamy smooth low-fat ricotta this healthy iced dessert is speckled with chunky pieces of cinnamon-flavoured honey-glazed oats and seeds.

SERVES FOUR TO SIX

INGREDIENTS

For the granola topping

30ml|2 tbsp SUNFLOWER OIL

30ml|2 tbsp CLEAR HONEY

30ml|2 tbsp SUNFLOWER SEEDS

30ml|2 tbsp SESAME SEEDS

30ml|2 tbsp FLAKED (SLICED) ALMONDS

30ml|2 tbsp HAZELNUTS, chopped

45ml|3 tbsp ROLLED OATS

2.5ml|½ tsp GROUND CINNAMON

For the ice cream

4 EGG YOLKS

75g|3oz|6 tbsp CASTER (SUPERFINE) SUGAR

5ml|1 tsp CORNFLOUR (CORNSTARCH)

2.5ml|½ tsp GROUND CINNAMON

300ml|½ pint|1¼ cups SEMI-SKIMMED (LOW-FAT) MILK

250g|9oz|generous 1 cup RICOTTA CHEESE

1 Preheat the oven to 180°C|350°F| Gas 4. Oil a baking sheet. To make the granola, warm the oil and honey together in a pan. Mix in the remaining ingredients then spread into a thin layer on baking sheet. Bake for 7–10 minutes, stirring once until evenly browned. Leave to cool and harden.

2 To make the ice cream, whisk the egg yolks, sugar, cornflour and cinnamon in a bowl until thick and pale.

3 Pour the milk into a heavy pan, bring it just to the boil, then gradually pour it on to the egg mixture, whisking constantly.

4 Return the mixture to the pan and cook over a gentle heat, stirring constantly until the custard thickens. Pour it back into the bowl, cover, leave to cool, then chill.

5 Add the ricotta cheese to the cooled custard and whisk together until smooth.

6 Pour the mixture into an ice cream maker and churn until it is thick. Crumble the granola into pieces and mix half into the ice cream. Churn until the ice cream is firm enough to scoop. Transfer the ice cream to a freezer container and freeze until required.

7 Serve the ice cream in tall glasses decorated with the remaining pieces of granola.

COOK'S TIP *The granola topping also tastes delicious sprinkled over other ice creams, or over bananas and yogurt for breakfast.*

Beetroot and Allspice Sorbet

Beetroot is surprisingly sweet, with a rich, earthy taste that's enhanced with mild spice. The resulting sorbet also make the most of the beetroot's lovely deep red colour.

SERVES SIX

INGREDIENTS

1kg|2¼lb RAW BEETROOT (BEETS)

150g|5oz|¾ cup CASTER (SUPERFINE) SUGAR

2.5ml|½ tsp GROUND ALLSPICE

150ml|¼ pint|⅔ cup WATER

1 Cut the beetroot into small pieces and push through a juicer to make 600ml|1 pint|2½ cups juice. If necessary, make up the quantity with water. Chill.

2 Put the sugar, allspice and water in a small pan and bring slowly to the boil, stirring until the sugar has dissolved. Remove the pan from the heat and cool.

3 Mix the beetroot juice with the syrup and pour into the ice cream maker. Churn until thick. Spoon into glasses or transfer to a freezer container and freeze until ready to serve.

COOK'S TIP *When preparing the beetroot (beets) for juicing, there is no need to trim or peel them first.*

Carrot, Apple and Ginger Water Ice

This sorbet not only tastes good, it's full of vital nutrients. Scrub the carrots but don't bother to peel the apples and ginger. Simply chop them all and push them through a juicer to make a smooth, tangy juice.

SERVES SIX

INGREDIENTS

175g|6oz|scant 1 cup CASTER (SUPERFINE) SUGAR

150ml|¼ pint|⅔ cup WATER

500g|1¼lb CARROTS, scrubbed

500g|1¼ lb COOKING APPLES

50g|2oz FRESH ROOT GINGER

1 Heat the sugar in a pan with the water until the sugar has dissolved. Bring to the boil and remove from the heat.

2 Roughly chop the carrots and apples. Finely chop the ginger. Push half the carrots and apples, then the ginger through the juicer, finishing with the remaining apples and carrots.

3 Pour the juice and syrup into the ice cream maker and churn to a thick slush. Spoon into glasses or transfer to a freezer container and freeze until ready to serve.

VARIATION *Instead of making a water ice, you could make a carrot, apple and ginger spritzer by omitting the sugar syrup and simply pushing the ingredients through a juicer and then adding soda water.*

COOK'S TIP *Fresh root ginger is one of the best natural remedies for indigestion and will help to settle an upset stomach, whether caused by food poisoning, motion sickness or morning sickness.*

Index

Picture credits

The publishers would like to thank the following companies for their kind permission to reproduce their photographs: p13 bottom, p14 top left, AKG Photographic Library; p9 left and right, Charmet; p10 right, bottom and left, p11 top right, bottom right and centre, p12 top right and centre, p13 top, Hulton Getty; p12 top left, The Advertising Archives; p8 top and bottom, private collection, The Bridgeman Art Library; p15 top and bottom, The Holmes Group.

Acknowledgements

The author and the publishers would like to thank Magimix, Gaggia, Philips and the Holmes Group for their invaluable help. The research, recipe development and photography for this book would not have been possible without the kind loan of their ice cream machines.

The authors would like to extend their special thanks to Julie Beresford, Annabel Ford and Kate Jay for their enthusiasm and help throughout the busy days of photography and to their families for trying every ice cream that has appeared in this book.

Notes

Bracketed terms are intended for American readers.

For all recipes, quantities are given in both metric and imperial measures and, where appropriate, in standard cups and spoons. Follow one set of measures, but not a mixture, because they are not interchangeable.

Standard spoon and cup measures are level. 1 tsp = 5ml, 1 tbsp = 15ml, 1 cup = 250ml/8fl oz.

Australian standard tablespoons are 20ml. Australian readers should use 3 tsp in place of 1 tbsp for measuring small quantities of gelatine, flour, etc.

American pints are 16fl oz/2 cups. American readers should use 20fl oz/ 2.5 cups in place of 1 pint when measuring liquids.

The recipes containing raw egg white should be avoided by those who are susceptible to infections, such as the very young and the elderly, but the rest can be enjoyed by all.

Medium (US large) eggs are used unless otherwise stated.

Main front cover image shows Christmas Pudding Ice Cream – for recipe, see pages 124–5.